Has any teaching been ....
most needed than the ....
means to be human? Fo....
the two basic questions '.... .... and Who am I?'
we become prisoners to either the fatalism of biological
determinism or the folly of believing we can invent our
own identity. Only the Christian view—that we are
created as God's image, marred by the fall, yet offered
restoration in Christ—is anchored to history, matches
reality, and offers us true and lasting dignity. It is a basic
key to the meaning of life.

In these pocket-sized, packed-full pages, Professor
David McKay has given us a wonderfully lucid, mind-
renewing exposition of biblical teaching. His splendid
book provides both the clarity and the stability we
desperately need. I wish every Christian would read it—
especially every young one.

Sinclair B. Ferguson
Chancellor's Professor of Systematic Theology,
Reformed Theological Seminary, Jackson, Mississippi

In this current moment of identity politics and, indeed,
identity chaos, anthropology is once again a most
pressing and important doctrine for all Christians, not
just as a theory or a subject for Sundays but as something
of immense practical importance in every sphere of life.
In this remarkably concise yet thorough book, David
McKay offers a fine, clear summary of the salient points
of biblical anthropology, integrating the doctrine into
the broader context of creation, of the covenants and of

Christology and salvation. This will be an excellent book for anyone wanting a fine introduction to the subject and a well-structured guide for personal study. This will help the reader think precisely about the subject.

Carl R. Trueman
Professor of Biblical and Religious Studies,
Grove City College, Pennsylvania

Questions about human origins, gender, authority, environment, work, leisure and so much more are pressing issues in our confused society. The reason is simple. We have abandoned the biblical doctrine of humanity and in its wake, chaos has ensued, both in the world around us and, sadly, in the church. 'What is man?' the Psalmist asks, and here, in these few pages, is the answer to that enigmatic question. David McKay's book on the doctrine of man is therefore most timely. Within the scope of a few hours reading, the basic essentials can be grasped with relative ease and considerable profit. Highly recommended for such a time as this. Buy it and read it and then buy another and give to a friend.

Derek W. H. Thomas
Senior Minister, First Presbyterian Church, Columbia,
South Carolina
Chancellor's Professor, Reformed Theological Seminary
Teaching Fellow, Ligonier Ministries

So many of the ethical issues and problems of today are rooted in a misunderstanding of who we are as men and women made in the image of God. In short compass David McKay helps us to recover our bearings with a fine summary of Biblical teaching on humanity: created, fallen, redeemed, and ultimately glorified. Here are the foundations of a better understanding of our nature and our purpose, and a reminder of our great salvation in Christ. I trust it will prove helpful to many.

Bill James
Principal, London Seminary, London

A CHRISTIAN'S POCKET GUIDE TO

HUMANITY

DAVID MCKAY

Created and Re-created

CHRISTIAN
FOCUS

Scripture quotations are from *The Holy Bible, English Standard Version®* (ESV®) Copyright © 2001 by Crossway, a publishing ministry of Good News Publishers All rights reserved. ESV Text Edition: 2011

Scripture quotations marked NIV are taken from the *Holy Bible, New International Version*. Copyright © 1973, 1978, 1984 by International Bible Society. Used by permission of Hodder & Stoughton Publishers, A member of the Hodder Headline Group. All rights reserved.

Scripture quotations marked NKJV are taken from the *New King James Version*. Copyright © 1982 by Thomas Nelson, Inc. Used by permission. All rights reserved.

paperback ISBN 978-1-5271-0640-6
epub ISBN 978-1-5271-0708-3
mobi ISBN 978-1-5271-0709-0

10 9 8 7 6 5 4 3 2 1
Published in 2021
by
Christian Focus Publications Ltd,
Geanies House, Fearn, Ross-shire,
IV20 1TW, Scotland, Great Britain
www.christianfocus.com

Cover design by Daniel Van Straaten

Printed by Nørhaven

CONTENTS

⚠ Warning
✎ Don't Forget
⑦ Stop and Think
⁂ Point of Interest

INTRODUCTION

The range of difficult ethical issues which Christians have to address is almost overwhelming. Some have been with us for centuries—war, poverty, economic exploitation and racism, to name just a few. Others are much more recent arrivals: euthanasia and genetic interventions would be significant examples. Several areas of heated ethical debate would not—could not—have been considered by earlier generations. Transgender issues and cloning, for instance, are throwing up questions that have never had to be asked or answered before. Now they cannot be avoided.

Often Christians are bewildered by the complexity of the issues involved and confused by the conflicting voices they hear, from friends, from the community around them, from the media and, sadly, from churches. We might well understand why some throw up their hands in despair and opt out, concluding that satisfactory answers cannot be found. Understandable, but unnecessary.

One of the main reasons for the confusion we encounter is the lack of a biblical understanding of what a human being is, or within the Church a loss of the understanding Christians once had. If we do not know what a human being is, how can we decide how to treat him or her? Is it right to clone a human being? Is it ever permitted to take a human life? Can a human being self-identify in any way he wishes? Are all human beings of equal value? We will not attempt to answer all of these questions, but we do aim to provide God-given fundamental principles regarding human nature that will enable you to find answers. At a more personal level, this study will also set out the basics of who we are and what, by God's grace, we can be—the basics of Christian discipleship.

No one would dispute that the questions are difficult, but Christians should not despair at finding answers. We believe that God is a God who has revealed Himself— in creation, in the human conscience, in the pages of the Bible and in the person of the Lord Jesus Christ. Crucially, God is a God who has spoken, using human language which is recorded in a book described by the Apostle Paul as 'God-breathed' (2 Tim. 3:16). What Scripture says, God says. That's why the *Westminster Confession of Faith* can refer to our final court of appeal in religious controversies as 'the Holy Spirit speaking in the Scripture' (I.x).

We are not left to our own intellectual resources: we have an authoritative revelation from God which addresses all areas of life and which is sufficient for every area of Christian discipleship. In the Bible we have an infallible source of 'wisdom', truth applied to life. That is precisely what we need.

But what is wisdom? John Calvin was correct when he wrote at the very beginning of his great work *Institutes of the Christian Religion* that 'true and sound wisdom consists of two parts: the knowledge of God and of ourselves'. The two, he argues, are intertwined. 'In the first place, no-one can look upon himself without immediately turning his thoughts to the contemplation of God…Again it is certain that man never achieves a clear knowledge of himself unless he has first looked upon God's face, and then descends from contemplating him to scrutinize himself.'[1]

In this short study our focus will be on what the Bible says about us—human beings made by and responsible to a sovereign Creator. We will begin with man as he came from the hands of the Creator, a sinless creature made for fellowship with God. The entrance of sin into God's good creation and its effects on human beings will have to be considered next. Having listened to this bad news, we will turn to the good news of God's gracious action to restore fallen men and women to fellowship with Himself through the redeeming work of the Lord Jesus Christ. The glorious consummation of that restoration project in the wonders of the new creation will be the

If the Bible is set aside, what resources have to be employed in order to try to understand human beings? How reliable are they?

final subject to occupy our attention. At every point knowledge of man and knowledge of God will be seen to be interwoven.

To grasp what the Bible says on these issues, we need to begin at the beginning, in Eden.

1

BEARING THE IMAGE OF GOD

In Psalm 8:4 (NKJV) David the psalmist asks rhetorically, 'what is man that you are mindful of him, and the son of man that you visit him?' To this fundamental question regarding human identity David gives an answer rooted in the creation account. Despite the smallness of human beings in God's universe, 'Yet you have made him a little lower than the heavenly beings and crowned him with glory and honour. You have given him dominion over the works of your hands; you have put all things under his feet' (vv. 5-6). The psalm takes us straight back to the account of human origins in Genesis 1-3.

We should note at this point that the Bible everywhere assumes that Adam and Eve are historical figures. There is, for example, no stage in the Genesis record where we can discern a transition from 'myth' (or some other such term) to 'history'. The record is all of a piece—it is all history. To this we must add Jesus' clear and straightforward acceptance of the historicity of the account of the origin of marriage given in Genesis 2 where He debates divorce with the Pharisees (Matt. 19:4-6; Mark 10:6-9). The Genesis record is quoted as fact: 'he who created them from the beginning made them male and female' (Matt. 19:4). The same outlook is evident in the Apostle Paul. Regarding Adam's creation he quotes Genesis 2:7, 'The first man Adam became a living being' (1 Cor. 15:45). The historicity of both Adam and Eve is accepted by Paul in 1 Timothy 2:13, 'Adam was formed first, then Eve' (with their fall mentioned in verse 14). Of greatest significance is the extended comparison of Adam and Christ in Romans 5:12ff. The one is as historical as the other.

If we accept the absolute authority of the Bible, we must accept the historicity of Adam and Eve. To deny

In Genesis 5:2 we read, 'Male and female he created them, and he blessed them and named them Man [Adam].' The name of the first man, Adam, is sometimes used to designate male human beings as distinguished from females (eg Gen. 2:22, 25) but sometimes also to designate the whole human race. This practice originates with God and so it should not be objectionable to us to refer to the human race as 'man'. That does not excuse insensitivity in our use of language so as to marginalise women, but 'man' as a term for the race is not just an accidental feature of Hebrew: it is God's naming activity and therefore good and holy.

that is to claim that Jesus and Paul (when he wrote Scripture) were fallible, and if on this issue, then on how many more? Adam is not some kind of mythological figure or an 'everyman' depicting the course that all men and women follow. He was an actual historical figure.

MAN'S UNIQUE ORIGIN

Two accounts of man's creation are provided in Genesis 1:26-27 and in Genesis 2:7, 21-23. These are complementary accounts, not contradictory. The first is part of a chronological account of the entire creation, whilst the second places the focus on man and shows how all that went before was designed to provide a suitable environment for human beings. Both accounts set out aspects of human uniqueness:

A Unique Consultation

In Genesis 1:26 God says, 'Let us make man in our image, after our likeness'. The plural 'us' and 'our' is best understood as an early indication of plurality within the one God whom the New Testament will reveal to be a Trinity, three 'persons' in one God. It is not, of course, an indication that God needed to discuss or weigh the pros and cons of creating man. It is a means of showing that man is the object of God's special care. As Calvin says, 'This is the highest honour with which he has dignified us'.[2]

A Unique Method

At each stage of the creation account we note God's direct command, such as 'Let there be light' (Gen. 1:3), 'Let the waters swarm' (v. 20). The creation of man is significantly different. In Genesis 2:7 we read, 'then the LORD God formed the man of dust from the ground and breathed into his nostrils the breath of life, and the man became a living creature.' However God may have acted in the rest of His creative work, there is in the creation of man an element of immediate personal involvement on the Lord's part. Whilst pre-existing material was used for the body, life is imparted in a unique way, God breathing the breath of life into Adam's nostrils.

A Unique Pattern

Living creatures and plants were created 'after their kind' (eg Gen. 1:11-12), indicating a range of divine patterns or blueprints for different groupings in the creation. With reference to man, however, we read in Genesis 1:26: 'Let us make man in our image, after our likeness'. We will have to consider what those expressions tell us about the human constitution, but we can say right away that they set man apart as the unique bearer of God's image. At the very least a special relationship with the Lord is indicated.

A Unique Constitution

Genesis 2:7 indicates that there are two elements in man's constitution. There is first the body, made up of 'dust from the ground'. A second element is breathed into Adam by God Himself, namely 'the breath of life'. In the case of man this expression seems to indicate something more than the 'life' possessed by the animals. This is reinforced by a verse such as Ecclesiastes 12:7: 'the dust returns to the earth as it was, and the spirit returns to God who gave it'. Two elements, a physical and a non-physical or spiritual are in view. In the New Testament the same view is stated in Jesus' words in Matthew 10:28 with reference to those 'who kill the body but cannot kill the soul'. What precisely 'spirit' and 'soul' refer to will be considered below.

A Unique Position

The structure of the creation account shows that man is the apex of God's creation, towards whom the rest of His work leads. Each part of creation has value in itself, but above all it provides a suitable environment for God's image-bearer. As Genesis 1:28 indicates, man was given 'dominion' over the creation, a concept which requires careful consideration. Under God, man stands

If we reject the historicity of Genesis 1-3 we also demolish the foundation of human uniqueness and create all kinds of problems, theological and ethical.

in a unique position in relation to the rest of creation: he is to be an agent of God's rule over creation, reflecting the likeness of the sovereign Creator. As it is sometimes put, man is created to be God's 'vicegerent' over creation.

WHY WAS MAN CREATED?

Before the creation of Adam and Eve God was not lonely, wondering how to express His loving nature. God did not have to create the human race, or indeed anything else. God is independent of everything outside Himself, a divine perfection that theologians designate 'self-existence' or 'aseity'. Furthermore since God's being is triune, one God in three persons, there was perfect fellowship within the Trinity in eternity before creation. This is evident in Jesus' reference to 'the glory that I had with you before the world existed' and 'my glory that you have given me because you loved me before the foundation of the world' (John 17:5, 24). Father, Son and Holy Spirit loved each other perfectly.

If God did not create man to satisfy any need or supply any lack that He experienced, why was man created? The ultimate answer must be that it was for God's own glory. That is the final explanation for all of God's acts. In them He displays His glory. Thus the human race has been created to manifest the glory of God. This is well summed up in the famous answer to Question 1 of the *Westminster Shorter Catechism*: 'Man's chief end is to glorify God and to enjoy him for ever'. Paul's words in 1 Corinthians 10:31 are a summons to fulfil the purpose of our existence: 'So, whether you eat or drink, or whatever you do, do all to the glory of God'. We cannot, of course, add to the infinite glory of God's being, but, as Puritan preacher Thomas Watson puts it, 'The glory we give God is nothing else but our lifting up his name in the world, and magnifying him in the eyes of others'.[3]

Although man did not satisfy a need in God, he was from the beginning the object of God's love and delight. Several striking texts which refer to His delight in His redeemed people can rightly be applied to His unfallen image-bearers in Eden too. As Isaiah 62:5 states, 'as the bridegroom rejoices over the bride, so shall your God rejoice over you'. Perhaps even more vivid is Zephaniah 3:17 'he will rejoice over you with gladness; he will quiet you by his love; he will exult over you with loud singing'. It is no exaggeration to suggest that when the Lord looked on Adam, part of a creation that was all 'very good' (Gen. 1:31), His heart sang.

At the centre of the biblical account of the creation of man is the Creator. The record is entirely God-centred as Moses under the direction of the Holy Spirit describes the origin of the human race and explains the purpose of human existence. This also provides clarity on two crucial issues: dignity and identity.

Dignity

Creation for the glory of God is the basis for the value and significance of human life. Human beings have value because God places value on them. Although God did not have to create man and does not need us for anything, nevertheless He has made us, we are 'fearfully and wonderfully made' (Ps. 139:14) and we are important to Him. As we shall see, our creation in God's image provides a further element in our significance. Human beings thus have a God-given dignity which must not be disregarded or minimised.

A proper biblical understanding of human dignity is necessary in the face of many of today's ethical challenges. To take one area by way of example, when confronted by advances in medical technology and treatment, such as developments in genetic therapies, it is crucial to ask whether these advances preserve or compromise human dignity. It is not the only factor to be assessed, but it is indispensable.

 When we fear pain and the painful process of dying, faith means that we can and ought to rely wholly on God to care, arrange and support in the ways He deems best for us. He can be trusted, even in our dying.

Identity

The creation account makes clear that it is God the Creator who determines human identity: it is God who tells us who we are. A token of this is provided by God's naming His creature 'Man' ('Adam', Genesis 5:2). The naming is an exercise of divine authority, providing not merely a convenient label but significantly a designation of the identity of this creature, 'Man'.

Issues of identity are among the most hotly debated in western societies. Who has the right to determine my identity? The answer now offered by many is that I alone determine my identity. This is clearly evident in discussions of sexuality, including homosexuality and transgenderism. Increasingly individuals are claiming the right to self-identify in any way they choose, regardless, for example, of their biology. Vaughan Roberts gets right to the heart of the matter: 'There's a deeply rooted conviction that everyone is free to define themselves as they wish, and no-one has the right to question that self-definition'.[4]

The apparent freedom that people have to define themselves is exactly that: apparent. It is in fact an illusion. The first attempt at self-definition was by Adam and Eve in Eden. Their assertion of supposed freedom was in fact rebellion against the Creator and left them cowering behind a tree, trying to hide from the sentence of the Creator who was now also their Judge. The pattern is endlessly repeated in human experience and in our present society self-definition has become a substitute for God-given dignity and identity.

In this context of widespread confusion regarding identity, Christians must be ready to assert, lovingly but clearly, that identity is not self-generated or self-invented, but is in fact given to us by God. It is our sovereign Creator who defines who and what we are. To deny this, in theory or in practice, is to fly in the face of what the Creator has determined and results inevitably in pain and sorrow for individuals and for societies as a whole. Apart from repentance and the grace of God in Christ, judgment must follow.

BODY AND SOUL

The emphasis of the Bible is on the unity of the human person. Although human nature comprises more than one element, a human being is nevertheless a unity. Thus in Genesis 2:7 Adam has a body taken from dust and into his nostrils the Lord God breathes 'the breath of life', with the result that 'the man became a living creature', a unified person with diverse elements functioning in harmony.

Every human act is regarded as an act of the whole person. Thus, according to 1 Corinthians 7:34 the unmarried or betrothed woman is to be concerned 'how to be holy in body and spirit' and in 2 Corinthians 7:1 we are encouraged to 'cleanse ourselves from every defilement of body and spirit'. Ultimately God's people will be unities of glorified bodies and perfect holy souls (1 Cor. 15:51-54).

Many existential and postmodern philosophies deny that there is such a thing as 'human nature' that endures through time, arguing instead that we are just bundles of successive experiences. The Bible's understanding of man is that each of us has an enduring nature and that there is an 'I' to whom God relates and who ought to relate to God.

We are, however, made up of two distinct elements. There is the material, physical element, the body, something we have in common, for example, with animals. There is also the non-material, spiritual element which the Bible designates the 'soul' or the 'spirit'. Human beings are composites of the material and the spiritual, body and soul/spirit.

Some theologians argue that soul and spirit are distinct, meaning that human beings consist of three elements: body, soul, and spirit. This view is called 'trichotomy'. Although there are a few verses that may seem to support this view (such as 1 Cor. 2:14-3:4 and 1 Thess. 5:23), the biblical evidence firmly supports dichotomy, the view that human nature is made up of two elements.

The biblical words for soul and spirit (*nephesh* and *ruach* in Hebrew and *psuchē* and *pneuma* in Greek) can refer to a person's life or to the whole person, but are often used to refer to the distinct, non-material part of human nature. When that is the case, it is significant that 'soul' and 'spirit' are used interchangeably.[5] Jesus, for example, says in John 12:27, 'Now is my soul troubled', whilst in a similar context he is said to be 'troubled in his spirit' (John 13:21). The same thing is evident in the parallel expressions (characteristic of Hebrew poetry) used in Mary's song in Luke 1:46-47, 'My soul magnifies the Lord, and my spirit rejoices in God my Saviour'.

This fundamental equation of soul and spirit is evident in many ways in the Bible. In Matthew 10:28, when Jesus warns 'And do not fear those who kill the body but cannot kill the soul. Rather fear him who can destroy both soul and body in hell,' it is evident that He is describing the whole person, with 'soul' designating the non-material element. This may be set alongside Paul's instruction in 1 Corinthians 5:5 regarding a sinning brother, 'you are to deliver this man to Satan for the destruction of the flesh, so that his spirit may be saved in the day of the Lord'. Again the entire person is in view and 'spirit' is sufficient to designate the non-material element. Similarly James states 'the body apart from the spirit is dead' (James 2:26).

Careful study of the biblical evidence indicates that everything the soul is said to do can also be predicated of the spirit, and vice versa. Those who hold to trichotomy often argue that 'soul' includes intellect, emotions and will, whilst 'spirit' is a higher faculty that comes alive at conversion. That would mean that the spirit is the part of man that relates to God most directly in prayer and worship. That view really cannot be defended from Scripture. To take just one issue, it is clear that man worships God with his soul: 'To you, O Lord, I lift up my soul' (Ps. 25:1), 'My soul magnifies the Lord' (Luke 1:46), 'And you shall love the Lord your God with all your heart and with all your soul and with all your mind and with all your strength' (Mark 12:30). It is not possible to distinguish soul and spirit.

What then are we to make of 1 Thessalonians 5:23: 'Now may the God of peace himself sanctify you completely, and may your whole spirit and soul and body be kept blameless at the coming of our Lord Jesus Christ'? It seems best to see Paul as piling up terms to stress the thoroughgoing nature of sanctification, much as we find Jesus doing with reference to loving God with 'heart ... soul ... mind' (Matt. 22:37), adding 'strength' in Mark 12:30. The Lord is not listing three or four elements of human nature but is rather demonstrating the comprehensive love that we ought to have for God.

How might a trichotomous view of man give rise to problems in understanding sin and salvation?

So what is the origin of the soul? The Bible offers no support for ideas of souls pre-existing bodies, so where do they come from? Two main views have been held by orthodox theologians. Both have arguments in their favour as well as objections that can be raised against them. We have space only to consider them briefly.

Traducianism

This is the view that the soul as well as the body is derived from our parents. Its defenders argue, for example, that God ceased His creative work on the sixth day (Gen. 2:2) and that descendants are said to be 'in the loins' of their fathers (eg Gen. 46:26, Heb. 7:9-10). In some sense, therefore, all human souls were present in Adam (a view termed 'realism').

Creationism

This is the view that each soul is the immediate creation of God. As God's creation it is perfectly holy but becomes sinful when united with the body. Reformed theologians often explain this on the basis of man's solidarity with

Adam in breaking the covenant in Eden (more on this below). Separate origins for body and spirit are indicated in a verse such as Ecclesiastes 12:7, 'the dust returns to the earth as it was, and the spirit returns to God who gave it'.

The issues involved are complex and we must be careful not to speculate beyond what God has revealed—always a sound rule in theology. On balance the creationist view seems to raise fewer problems.

Developments in brain science have led to much consideration of the relationship of the brain and the mind, usually without any reference to a spiritual dimension of human nature. It is suggested, for example, that when brains evolved to a certain level of complexity they generated what we call 'mind'. The development of artificial intelligence (AI) also feeds into these discussions. Christians need to have a clear grasp of the Bible's teaching about the spiritual dimension of human nature when the views widely accepted in our culture are basically materialistic.

THE IMAGE OF GOD

What, if anything, sets human beings apart from animals, particularly other primates? Is man nothing more than an 'intelligent ape', and perhaps not a particularly intelligent one in some respects? When arguments are being offered by lawyers seeking the recognition of rights for some primates analogous to human rights, we need a clear response. When radical ethicist Peter Singer of Princeton University claims that a healthy gorilla baby is of more value than a handicapped human baby, the questions are urgent in the extreme.

As with so much in relation to human nature, the key to a Christian response is to be found in the opening chapters of Genesis. Of crucial significance is God's deliberation in Genesis 1:26, 'Then God said, "Let us make man in our image, after our likeness."' No such deliberation preceded any other part of God's creative work. Something unique is about to happen. We have the result in verse 27, 'So God created man in his own image, in the image of God he created him; male and female he created them.'

So what does it mean to be made in the image of God? How does man bear the image of God? In the Old Testament 'image' is used of an object similar to something else and often representative of it, for example, the replicas of the tumours and the mice in 1 Samuel 6:5, 11. The term 'likeness' also denotes an object similar to something else, more often in contexts where similarity rather than representation is emphasised, for example the figures of the bulls under the bronze 'sea' in 2 Chronicles 4:4. Despite the efforts of some theologians, it is not possible to draw a clear distinction between image and likeness, arguing for example that one was lost in the Fall and the other not. Both terms would suggest to the first readers of Genesis that man was like God in some respects and also represented Him.

Different views have been held by theologians regarding the nature of the image of God. They fall into three broad categories:

1. Substantive views: these aim to find a particular quality or capacity possessed by man which constitutes the divine image. Often a faculty such as reason has been regarded as the image, not least since it sets human beings apart from animals.

2. Relational views: this approach is popular among some modern theologians with the image describing a being standing before God and capable of relating to Him. In his later writings German theologian Karl Barth regarded the image as rooted in the differentiation of male and female.

3. Functional views: these looked to something man does, rather than something man is. Most often man's exercise of dominion over the rest of creation has been thought of as the heart of what constitutes the divine image.

What is the best approach to understanding God's image in man? The wisest course is to begin with the God in whose image man is created. The phrase in Genesis 1:26 'Let us make man' contains the first hint of a truth which is gradually revealed as the Bible unfolds: within the one God, Creator and Lord, there is a plurality. Ultimately it is clear that this God is a Trinity, one God existing in three equal persons. From eternity this Triune God has been characterised by loving personal relationships among the three persons. In a most profound sense God is a relational God.

If man is made in the image of this Trinitarian relational God, we may say that he too is a relational being. In bearing the divine image man is made with a capacity for relationships, primarily with God his Creator, but also with other relational beings. Man is made for community, and the way in which that is expressed by means of a covenant will be considered in the next section.

The God who said, 'Let us make man in our image, after our likeness' delights to have fellowship in community with His human creatures. The relational capacity with which man has been created has implications for every aspect of his being. Bearing the image of God is a comprehensive blessing. We must therefore ask what kind of a creature man must be in order to fulfil the Creator's purpose for his life. In a very basic way we can note the following:

1. Spiritual elements: as well as having a physical body man has an immaterial soul/spirit by means of which he can relate to God in, for example, worship and prayer. This is the vital foundation for fellowship with God.

2. Intellectual elements: man has a capacity for reasoning, for abstract, logical thinking, not shared with other creatures. We may include here man's capacity for language use which is fundamental to relationships with God and with other human beings. Other intellectual elements would involve man's aesthetic capabilities, creating and enjoying beauty in, for example, art and literature. In this he reflects in a limited degree the creativity of God.

3. Moral elements: man was created with a capacity for knowing right and wrong, which is the basis of human moral accountability. Adam was created in a state of moral perfection, with a positive inclination to holiness. He possessed what is termed 'original righteousness', having a knowledge of God's righteous requirements, a will confirmed to God's holy will and a desire for what is pure and good. Man was oriented towards righteousness.

4. Relational elements: the fact that man is made for community with other human beings as well as with God is evident from the Lord's statement in Genesis 2:18, 'It is not good that the man should be alone. I will make a helper fit [or 'suitable'] for him.' God's immediate response to Adam's need for community was the creation of Eve and the institution of marriage. Man, however, is made for a wide range of relationships, in families, in society and in the Church. In each area he is to express the relational dimension of the divine image.

Is it possible that the image of God might somehow extend to the body? God does not have a physical body (John 4:24 and Luke 24:39), yet man is embodied and the people of God will have bodies for ever. At least in this present world bodies are essential for relationships and they enable us to do things that God, without a body, is able to do, such as seeing and hearing. Perhaps bodies allow the capacities of God to be translated into the terms of a physical world. Calvin believed that with respect to God's image in man 'there was no part of man, not even the body itself, in which some sparks did not glow.' (John Calvin, *Institutes*, I.xv.3)

We ought also to note the statement of Hebrews 1:3 regarding God the Son: 'He is the radiance of the glory of God and the exact imprint of his nature'. We may say that although man is made 'in the image of God', the Son is the image. The term in Hebrews 1:3 translated as 'exact imprint' is the word *charaktēr*, used of a precise reproduction of a portrait on, for example, a minted coin. The Son is the perfect revelation of what God is like.

Since the defaced image of God in sinful men and women is restored through the redeeming work of the Lord Jesus Christ, the Son of God incarnate, important insights into the image can be drawn from New Testament texts such as Colossians 3:10. Here Paul speaks of believers 'new self' (i.e. their new nature) as 'being renewed in knowledge after the image of its creator'. The word 'knowledge' refers to more than the possession of information about God. This is relational language. When God is said to 'know' his people (John 10:14; 2 Tim. 2:19), this indicates the establishment of a relationship with them. Increasing knowledge, as the image is restored, implies a deepening relationship with the Lord which results in a growing likeness to Him. At the last day 'we shall be like him, because we shall see him as he is' (1 John 3:2).

THE COVENANT IN EDEN.

What was the original relationship between the Triune God and man, His image bearer? With a few notable exceptions, most theologians in the Reformed tradition have held that the relationship that Adam and Eve enjoyed with God in Eden was a covenant relationship. Thus the fellowship between God and man was fundamentally covenantal.

At this point we had best spell out what is the biblical concept of a covenant.[6] It is a theme that runs all through the Bible, literally from Genesis to Revelation, and so it is of major significance. A useful, concise definition is provided by the great Scottish theologian Robert Rollock: 'The Covenant of God is a promise under some certain conditions.'[7] An examination of what the Bible says about covenant confirms Rollock's words.

A Promise

The covenant promise of God is best summed up in the words of Leviticus 26:12: 'And I will walk among you and will be your God, and you shall be my people'. Even when the precise form of words is not used, the basic covenant promise of the Lord is always the same (note, for example, Gen. 17:7; Exod. 6:7; Jer. 32:38). The same promise heralds the inauguration of the new creation in Revelation 21:3.

We need to stress that a covenant is first and foremost a promise, because it is easy to slip into thinking about God's covenant with man in coldly legal terms. Stirred by infinite love, God freely enters into covenant with His people. It is of course not an agreement between equals: God and man do not negotiate the terms of their relationship. The sovereign God decrees the terms of the covenant, and it is for man to accept them humbly and thankfully. The core of the covenant—its real heart—is nevertheless a loving, gracious promise.

Conditions

Without in any way compromising the sovereignty of the God who establishes His covenant, the Bible also stresses the necessity of a response of faith and obedience on the side of God's covenant partners. In every part of Scripture we encounter God's command to His people to keep the covenant He has made with them by their obedience to His commandments. We find the perfect biblical balance in, for example, Deuteronomy 7:9 with its reference to 'the faithful God who keeps covenant and steadfast love with those who love him and keep his commandments to a thousand generations'. The divine initiative must be met by a response to faith which, if it is genuine, inevitably results in willing and joyful obedience.

Love and Law

The biblical understanding of covenant holds together two vital things—love and law. God demonstrates His amazing love by entering into a covenant with man, and man in turn is to love the Lord and express his love in obedience shaped by God's law, which is itself a gift of divine love.

Some Reformed writers have been reluctant to speak of 'conditions' in relation to God's covenant, believing that such language compromises God's sovereignty and opens the door to human merit. Most, however, have understood that there are conditions in the covenant, which are fulfilled by God's enabling, and so all the glory is His.

Love and law are inextricably interwoven in the biblical concept of covenant. This is clear in the Lord's provision of the covenant of marriage which illustrates His relationship with His people. In Ezekiel 16:8, the Lord says to His people, 'I made my vow to you and entered into a covenant with you … and you became mine.' In a marriage a bond of love is forged—it is not a coldly legalistic contract—yet it nevertheless establishes a bond. Both parties undertake to fulfil commitments which have been motivated by love but which do not disappear if love should fade.

But is there a covenant in the Garden of Eden? The word 'covenant' is absent, but that does not necessarily mean that a covenant is absent. Most Reformed theologians have concluded that there is a covenant in Eden. One very significant text in this connection is Hosea 6:7 where the Lord, in exposing the sins of his people, says 'But like Adam they transgressed the covenant,'[8] strongly indicating that in Eden Adam was in covenant with the Lord.

The biblical balance of love and law needs to be carefully maintained. To neglect love makes a covenant a matter of grudging duty; to neglect law weakens commitment and leaves it without shape and direction.

Basic elements of a covenant can be discerned in Genesis 1-2. Adam's life in Eden is governed by God's word. Even in Paradise, before the Fall, there was a word-revelation from God alongside His revelation in creation. There is one crucial prohibition binding Adam: with reference to eating from 'the tree of the knowledge of good and evil' Adam is warned, 'in the day that you eat of it you shall surely die' (Gen. 2:17). It could not be simpler or clearer. Adam is left in no doubt about Gods' requirements and the consequences of disobedience. God's revelation of His will is to be met with obedience. We should also notice that in the early chapters of Genesis God's covenant name, 'the LORD', (Yahweh) is used, emphasising the covenant setting.

God's love and grace are abundantly evident in Eden. Adam and Eve were provided with the richest of environments which they could enjoy to the glory of their Creator. The entire creation was 'very good' (Gen. 1:31) in God's eyes and, with the creation of Eve, Adam lacked nothing. They had both been created in perfect holiness and enjoyed unspoiled fellowship with the Lord who evidently walked with them in the garden (cf Gen. 3:8). They were able to fulfil their covenant obligations.

What of God's promise? Although promises are not stated explicitly in Genesis 1-2, they are present by implication. If death was to be the consequence of disobedience, then obedience would entail the continuance of 'life', not just in the sense of biological existence but as 'life' in its fullest sense, life in covenant fellowship with God. What more could Adam and Eve desire? The relationship of love, trust and obedience for which they had been created would continue unspoiled. As a result God would be glorified and enjoyed, the 'chief end' of man according to the first question and answer of the Westminster Shorter Catechism.

Was there more? Many Reformed theologians have argued that Adam in Eden was placed 'on probation', tested for a limited time with respect to his obedience to God's commandment regarding eating from the tree of the knowledge of good and evil. Had Adam passed the 'test' it is argued, his state of holiness would have been confirmed permanently, so that he would be beyond the possibility of falling. Some even suggest he would have been elevated at once to heavenly glory.

When we compare these ideas with the biblical account it does seem that in many respects they are highly speculative. There is no indication that Adam was on probation for a set time or that he would receive some kind of 'higher' life had the test been passed. Dealing in 'what if' is a dangerous road to travel in biblical and theological study. Often appeal is made to what believers will ultimately receive 'in Christ' as if this tells us what Adam would have enjoyed had he not fallen. That, however, does not allow for the provision of greater blessings for the Lord's people as a result of the Saviour's work, greater blessings than if redemption had never been necessary. It seems safest to say that as long as Adam continued in faith and obedience he would have continued to enjoy unbroken fellowship with the Lord such as he already had.

ADAM OUR REPRESENTATIVE

There is therefore a covenant relationship between God and man in Eden. Theologians have applied various names to it, such as the Covenant of Creation or the Covenant of Nature. The commonest term is the Covenant of Works. Though some are troubled by the fear that this term suggests that man could accumulate merit by his works and place God under some obligation to bless, we may use the term as long as we remember that we are always 'unworthy servants' who 'have only done what is our duty' (Luke 17:10). God may, however, freely choose to bless obedience that is already owed to Him. It is for this reason that Adam's obedience in Eden is of such significance for him and for his descendants. This is appropriately called the Covenant of Works.

What is clear in Scripture is that Adam in Eden acted not only as an individual but also as a representative of the whole human race that would derive its existence from him. In the language of 1 Corinthians 15:22 we are 'in Adam': there is a covenantal union between Adam and his descendants.

This fact became clear in the way in which the relationship between fallen Adam and his descendants is described in several New Testament passages. We will look at these more closely when we consider the Fall

We must never think that our obedience places God in our debt. Any reward He bestows on the obedience we owe is a token of His love and grace.

in chapter 2 and the work of Christ in chapter 3, but they are also important for understanding the pre-Fall arrangements put in place by the Lord.

Thus death, in its fullest sense of ruptured fellowship with God, is the lot of every human being, not through personal repetition of the pattern of temptation and fall of Adam in Eden, but as a result of a spiritual—a covenantal—solidarity with Adam. As 1 Corinthians 15:22 states, 'in Adam all die'. In this verse a vitally important parallel between Adam and Christ is set out: 'as in Adam all die, so in Christ all will be made alive' (NIV). Just as those who are in covenant union with Christ receive the benefits of His redemptive work, so those who are in covenant union with Adam receive the poisoned fruit of his disobedience. This is worked out in detail by Paul in Romans 5:12-19.

Adam is therefore to be thought of as the head and representative of the entire human race in the Covenant of Works. Whatever he did by way of obedience or disobedience would affect all his descendants. Complaints of unfairness—'I had no choice in this'—are beside the point: the Creator had the right to make whatever arrangements He chose for His creatures. We are 'in Adam' and his actions implicate us all.

 The covenantal, representative principle that applies to Adam also applies to Christ in his provision of salvation. If we have problems accepting the first, we should have problems accepting the second.

A GOD-GIVEN MANDATE

Life in Eden was not designed by God to be one of idleness, nor was Adam left to figure out how to occupy his time. By His Word-revelation, the covenant Lord told the man and his wife how to live.

In the widest sense Adam and Eve were to submit all their thinking and all their activity to the will of God. The omniscient God is the source of all knowledge, and so if man is to know anything truly he has to 'think God's thoughts after him'. In order to interpret the world correctly he has to base his thinking on God's revelation both in creation and in His Word. Man's knowledge is to be a reflection of the knowledge of his covenant Lord. In Eden, Adam and Eve were to use all their God-given intellectual capacities to engage with the rich environment in which the Creator had placed them.

More specifically God gave to man a twofold mandate:

1. Fruitfulness. 'Be fruitful and multiply and fill the earth and subdue it' (Gen. 1:28). The life-giving Creator commands His image-bearers to be life-givers, according to their finite human capacities. By God's enabling the human race is to grow, expand its range and flourish.

2. Dominion. 'Have dominion over the fish of the sea and over the birds of the heavens and over every living thing that moves on the earth' (Gen. 1:28). This command has sometimes been portrayed as offering justification for the destructive exploitation

of creation and blame for environmental damage has been laid at the Bible's door. Wrongly so. Adam was not given a license for the selfish exploitation of creation but was rather placed in Eden to be a steward in the service of the Creator, accountable to Him.

The kind of work involved in exercising dominion is indicated in Genesis 2:15: 'The LORD God took the man and put him in the garden of Eden to work it and keep it [NIV 'take care of it']'. The mandate involved both conservation and development. Using their God-given capacities Adam and his wife are to develop the potential of the creation in ways that enhance rather than harm it. Covenantal obedience would be expressed in all kinds of cultural, scientific and technological activities carried out to the glory of God. This has been referred to by terms such as 'the cultural mandate' and 'the civilizational mandate'. Bearing the image of God entails creative work.

Adam's role in Eden has sometimes been summed up in terms of a threefold 'office' which reflects the threefold office of Christ the Redeemer: prophet, priest and king.

As prophet, Adam received God's revelation and had the privilege and responsibility of communicating it faithfully to others, beginning with his wife Eve.

As priest, Adam was to live all of life in submission to God's will for God's glory, and in particular he was to lead his family in the worship of God. In a profound sense the whole Garden of Eden was a sanctuary with Adam as priest.

As king, Adam was to exercise godly dominion over the creation, reflecting the kingship of his Creator. His naming the animals (Gen. 2:19-20) was an exercise of kingly authority.

MAN AS MALE AND FEMALE

In Eden, Adam and Eve were in a covenant relationship with their Creator God. That covenant was reflected and illustrated in the relationship in which God placed them with one another, namely marriage. In response to His own statement that 'It is not good that the man should be alone' (Gen. 2:18), God created Eve from Adam's own body, 'a helper fit for him' (v. 18). Here is the origin of the 'one flesh' relationship that is marriage. That this is a covenant relationship is evident from a text such as Malachi 2:14-16, especially verse 14, 'she is your companion and your wife by covenant'. The Lord establishes a relationship of love which also entails obligations (law).

Marriage is thus a 'creation ordinance' established at the very origin of the human race. It is not the only way in which male and female are to relate for the glory of God: there are numerous God-honouring relationships between men and women. We are not to overvalue or undervalue marriage. If it is God's will for a particular man and a particular woman to marry, then the result is a beautiful relationship which, as Paul later shows, reflects the relationship of Christ and His Church (Eph. 5:22ff). For others marriage is not God's will. It would be an obstacle to their serving God in the way He has planned, as Paul shows in 1 Corinthians 7:29-35, and so 'there are eunuchs who have made themselves eunuchs for the sake of the kingdom of heaven', as Jesus says in Matthew 19:12. Those who are not married, in the will of God, have not 'missed God's best' as it is sometimes foolishly said.

Two fundamental principles regarding the biblical pattern for marriage need to be emphasised.

 The Bible nowhere countenances the idea that marriage may be between individuals of the same sex. It is from the outset between a man and a woman. Even the cases of polygamy that were sometimes tolerated in the Old Testament brought nothing but conflict and sorrow.

Fundamental Equality.

Male and female are equally made in the image of God. Despite what some theologians have suggested, there is no indication in the creation account that the male is somehow more of an image-bearer than the woman. Thus both are equally valuable in the sight of God, and indeed the creation of the two sexes serves to exhibit the richness of the image of God.

In marriage this fundamental equality must be maintained against all cultural and philosophical pressures to the contrary. The biblical teaching stands in judgment over all views that exalt one sex over the other, whether patriarchal conservatism or feminist radicalism. Whatever a culture may say, it is God's evaluation that shows how male and female are to be viewed.

Male Headship

The terminology of 'headship' in marriage has in recent times become highly controversial and has generated a vast literature from widely differing points of view. We can do no more than scratch the surface here.

Belief in male headship in marriage derives from passages such as 1 Corinthians 11:3, 'I want you to understand that the head of every man is Christ, the head of a wife is her husband, and the head of Christ is God', and Ephesians 5:23, 'For the husband is the head of the wife even as Christ is the head of the church, his body, and is himself its Saviour'. The Trinitarian context of Paul's words indicates that the issue is not superiority and inferiority: Christ and the Father are equal in all respects. This is often referred to as the 'essential Trinity', God as He is in Himself. There is, however, an order in the relationship within the Trinity, expressed in the works of God. This is often referred to as the 'economic Trinity', the same Triune God as He relates to His creatures. This is an order that is not reversible, nor are the persons interchangeable. So it is in marriage.

Some theologians have sought to argue that the word used by Paul, translated 'head' is in fact to be understood as 'source' and carried no implications of authority, a radical rewriting of the traditional understanding of headship. Despite the various arguments offered in defence of this revisionist view, exhaustive linguistic investigation by scholars such as Wayne Grudem has demonstrated that as the word *kephalē* was used before and during the New Testament period, it cannot be emptied of ideas of authority.[9]

But perhaps this situation pertains after the Fall? Some theologians suggest it is the entrance of sin into God's good creation that has brought about male 'headship' over the wife. It has even been regarded as satanic in origin. Without denying that sin has a profound effect on marriage, as we will see in the next chapter, it has to be said that distinctions between male and female and exercise of male headship in marriage were present before the Fall.

The order of creation is not insignificant: Paul builds a theological point on 'Adam was formed first, then Eve' in 1 Timothy 2:13. The serpent's approaching Eve first (Gen. 3:1) can be seen as an attempt to undermine and even reverse God's order in creation. Eve was tempted to take on a position of headship.

The designation of Eve as 'a helper' in Genesis 2:18 is also illuminating. We have to recognise that often in the Old Testament a 'helper' is greater or more powerful than the one helped. It is a term applied even to God, for example in Exodus 18:4 and Psalm 121:1-2. Nevertheless, a helper always takes on a subordinate position in relation to the one helped, thus showing the gracious condescension of God in being the 'helper' of

His people. We are dealing with order and with roles, not with intrinsic value.

Crucial in this regard is the covenant headship of Adam discussed above. It is 'in Adam' that all die (1 Cor. 15:22), not 'in Adam and Eve'. The ultimate responsibility for the Fall is placed at Adam's door: he alone is answerable for his actions with regard to his descendants.

Headship and consequent submission (Eph. 5:22-24) must be seen in the context of self-giving covenant love, mirroring Christ and the Church. The entrance of sin into the good creation of God has done great damage to the marriage relationship, both headship and submission. But neither is the result of sin. As Paul shows in Ephesians 5:22ff, by God's grace in Christ they may both be restored to a more faithful representation of the Creator's intention.

The perfection of Eden, however, did not last, and so we now turn our attention to the Fall.

In what ways does the creation pattern for marriage differ from what we see around us in contemporary culture?

2

RAVAGED BY SIN

The perfection of Eden lasts for only two chapters of the Book of Genesis. At the beginning of chapter 3 an evil creature is at work, using the serpent as his mouthpiece, and within a few verses Adam and Eve have disobeyed God and sin has entered the world which God had created 'very good'. There is no indication of how much time has passed between Genesis 2:25 and Genesis 3:1, but it may not have been very long.

The account of the Fall of the human race into sin provided in Genesis 3, set in the wider context of God's revelation in Old and New Testaments, is crucial to understanding why the world is as it is, and why human beings are as they are. Without a proper understanding of the disease that afflicts us, we will never be ready to accept the medicine of the gospel.

GENESIS THREE IS HISTORY

The idea that Genesis 3 contains a historical record of what happened to two people at the beginning of human history seems utterly ridiculous to many, including numerous professional biblical scholars. Surely this is just the Israelite version of the myth of 'paradise lost' common to most primitive cultures? Should Adam not be viewed as a sort of 'everyman' figure whose actions and fate depict the sad course which most of us follow? For some, Genesis 3 provides an excuse for keeping people in subjection to religious authorities who offer the solution to 'sin', thus denying them the freedom to realise their autonomous, free potential as human beings. Is Genesis 3 not in fact life-denying mythology that flies (vainly) in the face of evolutionary progress?

If we accept the authority of the Bible as 'God-breathed' Scripture, using Paul's terminology in 2 Timothy 3:16, we must reply that Genesis 3 is indeed history. At the beginning of chapter 1 we noted how Jesus and the apostles accepted the historicity of the creation account in Genesis 1-2. Moving to Genesis 3 changes nothing. The other biblical writers accepted the historical accuracy of the account of the Fall.

In Hosea 6:7, a verse to which we will return shortly, we read, 'But like Adam they transgressed the covenant'.

Clearly a specific, historical act on Adam's part is in view. In the New Testament the historicity of Adam is made unmistakeably clear. Paul builds a complex argument in Romans 5 on the assumption that Adam is as much a historical figure as is the Lord Jesus Christ. In Romans 5:12 Paul states that 'sin came into the world through one man, and death through sin' and in verse 16 he refers to 'the judgment following one trespass [which] brought condemnation'. The whole argument, with the parallels and contrasts between Adam and Christ, requires the historicity of Adam. This is reinforced by 1 Corinthians 15:21-22 ('by a man came death … in Adam all die'). We should also note 2 Corinthians 11:3, 'the serpent deceived Eve' and 1 Timothy 2:14, 'Adam was not deceived, but the woman was deceived'. In Genesis 3 we are dealing with historical events.

THE ORIGIN OF EVIL

So where did evil come from? If God made the world, indeed the entire universe, 'very good' (Gen. 1:31), how could evil gain a foothold and do the tremendous damage that the Genesis account records? That is a question that has exercised the greatest theological and philosophical minds for centuries, and it is not a question purely for dispassionate scholarly discussion. When God's people see the wickedness and the suffering that are so abundant in the world, or when they or their loved ones experience these things personally, the question of the origin of evil inevitably arises. People of other faiths and of none wrestle with the same issue and may use it as a stick with which to beat Christians.

Despite the centuries of debate, the origin of evil remains a mystery. Often attempts to explain its origin have really amounted to no more than descriptions of its nature: the 'what', rather than the 'why'. The Bible does not explain where evil comes from. In Genesis 3:1 mention is made of 'the serpent' which functions as a mouthpiece for Satan. Evil is already present in God's good creation, having entered the angelic world first. Recognising the presence of evil in 'that ancient serpent, who is called the devil and Satan' (Rev. 12:9), however takes us no closer to understanding the source of that evil. We are left to wonder how sin could prove attractive to unfallen human beings or to unfallen angels, and we must accept that it is a mystery. We do not need to understand the origin of evil, and in all probability if the Lord were to explain it, our little minds could not comprehend what He was telling us.

We do, nevertheless, need to hold firmly to two fundamental truths regarding the entrance of sin into God's good creation. The first truth is that in no sense is God the author of sin. That is the unwavering universal testimony of the entire Bible. The Lord is 'of purer eyes than to see evil and cannot look on wrong' (Hab. 1:13). To concede that in any sense, however limited, God is the author of sin brings the whole system of biblical theology crashing down.

The second fundamental truth is that the entrance of sin into the world, in particular the Fall of man, is not outside the control of God. There is no suggestion anywhere in Scripture that the sin of Satan or of Adam took God by surprise or was beyond His control. He remains sovereign even in these events. Whilst this may leave difficult theological and philosophical questions about God's relationship to evil, we cannot abandon commitment to God's absolute sovereignty and opt for a 'limited' God who does His best.

What are the consequences of abandoning either of these fundamental truths?

THE RECORD OF THE FALL

The Westminster Confession of Faith sums up the fall of man in these terms:

> Our first parents, being seduced by the subtilty and temptation of Satan, sinned, in eating the forbidden fruit. This their sin, God was pleased, according to His wise and holy counsel, to permit, having purposed to order it to His own glory.

Satan's initial approach, according to Genesis 3:1, is to Eve. Why might that be the case? There is no indication that there was some inherent weakness in the woman that rendered her more likely to fall than Adam. It may be that Satan considered that Eve would provide an easier route to the heart of Adam for his temptation, or it may be that since Eve had not received God's prohibition on eating from the tree of the knowledge of good and evil directly (Gen. 2:17), doubts and questions about it might be more easily aroused in her mind. It could be that, if Adam had some understanding of his covenant headship, he might have had a greater sense of responsibility for his actions, although the apparent lack of resistance to taking the fruit from Eve might call that into question. The fact is that we don't know why Satan adopted this approach and further speculation is futile.

The process of temptation recorded in Genesis 3 is significant, the tactics are those Satan often uses. He begins by questioning God's command—'Did God actually say…?' He suggests that this single prohibition is an unreasonable restriction on human freedom. As Eve weighs up this question, the tempter has gained a foothold. When Eve replies she adds an element to the prohibition which God had not stated: 'neither shall you touch it' (v. 3). She exaggerates the restriction which God has placed on them. The focus is not now on the almost limitless freedom which the good Creator has bestowed on man but rather on the single restriction, and indeed on an exaggerated version of it.

At this point Satan strikes hard. His next move is an open denial of the truth of God's word, 'You will not surely die' (v. 4), a blatant lie which opens the way for a falsification of God's character and motives. Satan portrays the Lord as selfish and fearful of His creatures, determined to keep them in a subordinate position, their potential unfulfilled. Now comes the heart of the temptation, the astounding claim, 'You will be like God' (v. 5). What more attractive offer could there be?

In verse 6 the transaction is completed. The appeal of the fruit to the senses (food and aesthetic pleasure) and to the spirit ('to be desired to make one wise') reinforce the offer of equality with God. Eve eats and Adam, with a clearer understanding of the issues, follows her into sin. Disaster has struck.

How does Satan continue to use these same tactics in presenting temptation to men and women? How have you experienced this?

THE FUNDAMENTAL SIN

What, then, was the nature of that first, that fundamental sin? There were, no doubt, various elements involved, each playing a part in the fall from perfect holiness. It has often been argued, especially by Roman Catholic theologians, that the fundamental issue was pride. Reformed theologians have been more inclined to argue that the first step into sin was unbelief, expressed particularly in relation to God's threat that 'in the day that you eat of it you shall surely die' (Gen. 2:17). This unbelief seems to have expressed itself in doubts about God's desire and provision for the very best for His image-bearers.

Whatever the precise contributing factors, however, we can say that the fundamental sin in Eden was covenant-breaking. If the argument of chapter 1 is correct, Adam and Eve stood in a covenant relationship to the Lord, then their eating the fruit forbidden by their covenant God was a violation of that covenant bond. The first sin broke the Covenant of Works.

The obligation resting on Adam in the Covenant of Works was obedience, loving and willing, to the love which the Lord lavished on him daily in the perfect environment of Eden. When Adam sinned, instead of submitting every thought to God's revelation, he was asserting the autonomy and sufficiency of his own thinking in defiance of God and in the depths of his being he was rebelling against God. In a moment Adam moved from being a covenant-keeper to being a covenant-breaker.

In Eden Adam refused to accept God's covenant kingship over him and attempted instead to make himself king. The truth was that he was actually pledging his allegiance to the dominion of Satan, and far from being autonomous he was a miserable slave. He really was now in 'the dominion of darkness' (Col. 1:13, NIV). In a sense Adam had made himself God, or at least he had tried to put himself in the place of God, just as the tempter had suggested. In at least three ways Adam's sin denied God His rightful place.[10]

1. Sin struck at the basis of knowledge. Adam's action was a practical denial of God's role as the source of truth. Adam set himself up as the arbiter of truth, trying to make God answerable to him.

2. Sin struck at the basis of ethics. Adam refused to accept the will of God as the standard of right

and wrong, profitable and harmful. Human reason became the moral arbiter.

3. Sin struck at the basis of self-understanding. Adam refused to allow God to define his identity—a dependent creature. He wanted to assert his independence.

THE IMMEDIATE CONSEQUENCES OF SIN

The consequences of covenant-breaking become clear when 'they heard the sound of the Lord God walking in the garden in the cool of the day' (Gen. 3:8). The life of the covenant is no more. Instead we see:

1. A sense of guilt and shame. Note verse 7: 'the eyes of both were opened, and they knew that they were naked'. This reflects a consciousness of the pollution that sin has brought. What had not been an issue before now brings deep discomfort.

2. Loss of friendship with God. In place of the loving covenant fellowship with the Lord for which they had been created, now they 'hid themselves from the presence of the Lord God' (v. 8). God is now a righteous Judge to be feared.

3. Disruption of their relationship with one another. In place of loving unity there is anger and blame-shifting, ultimately onto God ('The woman whom you gave,' v. 12). Sin has driven Adam and Eve apart, creating self-centred competition.

The universality and pervasiveness of sin is evident in the sentences God passes on Satan, on the woman and on man (Gen. 3:14ff), sentences which begin to show that sin does not affect only the first two human beings.

As far as Satan is concerned, God's words in Genesis 3:14-15 contain both judgment on the tempter and grace for those he has deceived. The words relating to the serpent—'on your belly you shall go and dust you shall eat' (v. 14)—make the serpent's means of locomotion along the ground symbolic of the divine curse. Satan himself is clearly in view in verse 15, 'I will put enmity between you and the woman, and between your offspring and her offspring'. God promises spiritual warfare between the offspring of the serpent, those under the dominion of Satan in rebellion against God, and the offspring of the woman, those who by God's grace receive His promise of salvation in faith and become citizens of His kingdom. History from this point on will be characterised by the unfolding of a spiritual antithesis between the servants of Satan and the servants of God.

Only God's grace could change a fallen, rebellious sinner into a child of God, and the latter part of verse 15 begins to speak of the operation of that grace which provides hope for Adam, Eve and the human race. The warfare foretold comes to a focus in individual combat between Satan and the 'offspring' (or 'seed') of the woman. The result will be a decisive victory for the seed of the woman: 'he shall bruise your head and you shall bruise his heel'. The tempter will be conquered, albeit at a cost to the seed of the woman. In the full light of the

New Testament it is evident that the seed of the woman is the Lord Jesus Christ who wins the redemptive victory at the cross and the empty tomb. Thus even in the curse of Genesis 3:14-15 there is a promise of grace, victory and salvation, the first gospel promise.

God's sentence on the woman is pronounced in verse 16. There are profound effects on her physical life: 'pain in childbearing'. That which is a blessing and a means of carrying out the Creator's mandate to fill the earth (Gen. 1:28) also brings pain and suffering. In addition the Creator's perfect pattern for marriage is profoundly damaged by sin.[11] God says to Eve, 'Your desire shall be for your husband', indicating that in place of willing submission to Adam's covenant headship, Eve will have a wrongful desire to usurp authority over her husband. The other element of the curse is contained in the words 'he shall rule over you'. In place of loving headship Adam will exercise harsh, selfish dominion, misusing the role God had assigned him. The previous harmony has gone, the 'battle of the sexes' has begun.

Adam's 'ruling' over Eve is part of God's sentence on sin: it is not a mandate for men to exercise self-centred dominion over women.

God's sentence on the man has several dimensions. The perfection of Eden has been destroyed and even the material environment is caught up in the consequences. God says, 'cursed is the ground because of you' (v. 17), with the result that it produces 'thorns and thistles', harmful, resistant to man's work. These surely symbolise all the harmful aspects of a damaged creation, including diseases and 'natural disasters'. In Romans 8:20-21, Paul refers to 'futility' and 'bondage to decay' with reference to the creation and states clearly that these are the result of God's judicial action, not merely natural consequences.

A consequence of the impact of human sin on the creation is stated in verse 17, 'in pain you shall eat of it all the days of your life'. Significantly the same word for 'pain' used here also occurs in verse 16 regarding post-Fall childbirth. Instead of the delightful and satisfying work of paradise, Adam will now have to labour to gain a living from the soil. The exercise of dominion has become a struggle against a resistant earth. Whilst there is again continuity with pre-Fall activity, there is also profound discontinuity because of sin. Even in the curse there is a measure of blessing, as God does not punish man as severely as He might have done. Despite the labour required, the ground will still supply man's needs. In wrath God remembers mercy.

The sentence on man finally becomes a death sentence. God states that 'you are dust and to dust you shall return' (v. 19). Physical death is certainly in view, but more is intended. God had threatened 'in the day you eat of it you shall surely die' (Gen. 2:17) and Adam did indeed die as soon as he ate. This is clear when we see the wide-ranging significance of death in Scripture. Adam died spiritually when fellowship with God was broken—'life' is knowing God personally (John 17:3). He also died judicially, separated from God, standing under the curse of the broken covenant (Eph. 2:1). He would die physically, body and soul separating unnaturally, and the process of dissolution had begun. Unless God intervenes he will die eternally, the 'second death' of Revelation 20:14. As Paul says in Romans 5:12, 'sin came into the world, and death through sin'

Finally God banishes Adam and Eve from Eden (v. 22-24) to prevent access to 'the tree of life'. There is, however, mercy in God's action as well as judgment. The cherubim and the flaming sword 'guard the way to the tree of life'. There is a way back, but only on the basis of the redeeming work of the seed of the woman.

UNITY IN ADAM

So how does this ancient history relate to us? Far from being a matter of antiquarian curiosity, the account provided in Genesis 3, together with its outworking in the rest of the Bible, explains all the essentials regarding why we are the kind of people we are and why the world is in the mess it is. Genesis 3 is of the greatest significance for all of us.

In reality Genesis 3 is our history, not just that of the first two human beings. When Adam fell the result was a disaster for the whole human race. As the *Shorter Catechism* puts it, 'The covenant being made with Adam, not only for himself, but for his posterity; all mankind, descending from him by ordinary generation, sinned in him, and fell with him in his first transgression' (Q 16). In the quaint language of the *Larger Catechism* question 22, Adam was 'a publick person'.

We noted in chapter 1 that according to the arrangements put in place in Eden, Adam was the representative of the whole human race in the Covenant of Works. What, if anything, of this situation was known to Adam, we cannot tell. It was, however, God's sovereign disposition. What Adam did thus implicated all of his descendants 'by ordinary generation', that is by the usual process of human procreation, Jesus Christ being the single exception.

The covenantal link between Adam and the rest of the human race is essential for a biblical understanding of sin. Human beings do not simply sin individually, following their own personal path of temptation and fall. There is a spiritual solidarity between Adam and his descendants, a solidarity in sin.

Our unity in Adam is made starkly clear in a text such as 1 Corinthians 15:22, 'as in Adam all die, so also in Christ shall all be made alive'. The second part of the verse is a salutary reminder that if we have difficulties with Adam's representative covenant role, we ought, to be consistent, to have difficulties with Christ's representative covenantal role in salvation. All who are 'in Adam' die—there are no exceptions.

In Romans 5:12ff Paul gives extended consideration to the parallels and differences between Adam and Christ. What Paul has to say about Adam in these verses takes us to the heart of human sinfulness. In verse 12 Paul begins with a bold statement: 'sin came into the world through one man, and death through sin, and so death spread to all men because all sinned'. The presence of sin in human lives is traced back to its root in the sin of Adam. In verse 19 Paul expands on this thought: 'by the one man's disobedience the many were made sinners'. It is on the basis of Adam's action that men and women are constituted sinners in God's sight.

There can only be one consequence of the link between Adam and his descendants. As Paul puts it, 'For the judgment following one trespass brought condemnation' (Rom. 5:16) and 'because of one man's trespass, death reigned through that one man' (v. 17). In unity with Adam the human race is constituted and declared guilty before God and justly condemned to death. Human nature is corrupted at its roots and all men stand guilty before the just Judge. As David says in Psalm 14:1 (NIV): 'They are corrupt, their deeds are vile; there is no-one who does good.' Without for a moment excusing the individual sinner, Scripture regards the link with Adam as of fundamental importance. Death in all its aspects is the result of Adam's sin for all 'in him'. As John Murray expresses it,

> Not only did death rule over them, not only did they come under the sentence of condemnation, but sinnership itself became theirs by reason of the sin of Adam.[12]

But why should Adam's sin have such devastating effects on those who were not present in Eden? Some theologians, including Reformed theologians like W. G. T. Shedd, have sought the connection in our physical descent from Adam. Shedd argues that human nature forms a numerical unity and so all of Adam's descendants were 'really' present with him in Eden. Despite eminent names who support it, this view is not convincing and causes more problems than it solves.

On this view it is difficult to see why only Adam's first sin affects the descendants 'really' present in him, and also why we do not inherit the guilt of the sins of all our ancestors.

To understand our unity with Adam and our solidarity in sin with him we must rather think covenantally. We have previously shown that Adam stood before God as the representative of the whole human race in the Covenant of Works. Now we see the sad consequences that follow when our representative sins. While Adam stood, we stood; when Adam fell, we also fell. The action of our representative implicated us all.

In theological language we say that the sin of Adam in eating the forbidden fruit was 'imputed' to all those descended from him in the ordinary way of human reproduction. By the covenant they are 'in Adam' and as a consequence they have his sin imputed to them and they die (1 Cor. 15:22). To say that sin is 'imputed' is to say that it is 'charged to our account'—it stands against us as if we had committed that first sin with Adam.

The exact nature of this imputation has been a matter of debate among theologians equally committed to a covenantal understanding of our unity in Adam, so we need to handle the subject humbly and carefully, trying not to speculate beyond what God has revealed in His Word.

All agree that every human being is born with a corrupt and sinful nature because of the covenantal link with Adam. Thus far there is agreement. Some then argue that our guilt before God the Judge is the result of that inborn corruption: we are guilty because corrupt. This is known as 'mediate imputation' and it begins with our corruption and on that basis regards us as guilty. The other main contender in the field is known as 'direct (or immediate) imputation'. This argues that because Adam was head of the whole human race in the Covenant of Works, his disobedience constituted all his descendants as sinners, appealing to a verse like Romans 5:19. As a result his guilt is imputed to them because of the covenant link. Only that first act of disobedience on Adam's part is relevant to the covenant and only it is imputed to his descendants. The result is that all are born in a corrupt, sinful condition. Direct imputation reverses the order adopted in mediate imputations and bases corruption on guilt, not vice-versa.

After reading that last paragraph, your head may be spinning and you may be wondering whether it really matters which view of imputation we adopt. Equally orthodox theologians and biblical scholars differ on the matter and that should make us careful about rushing to unduly dogmatic pronouncements. It is important, however, that our theology be as close to God's revelation as possible. Understanding the nature of our sinful condition as accurately as possible is very important, not least because it has implications for how we understand the work of Christ. It seems to me, therefore, that immediate imputation is the better view: our corrupt sinful condition flows as a consequence of our legal standing before God as covenant breakers guilty in Adam. As Paul states in Romans 5:19, 'by the one man's disobedience the many were made sinners'. One act of rebellion brought disaster on the whole race.

THE HUMAN CONDITION

If we are to understand human beings and, indeed, the world post-Fall, 'east of Eden' (Gen. 4:16) we need to look beyond individual sinful actions to the sin that is rooted in human nature and human hearts. We must recognise that the root problem is not 'sins' but 'sin'. If we fail to understand this, we may slip into believing that the solution to the problem of human sinfulness consists in dealing one by one with separate sinful habits and actions, thereby leaving the root of sin untouched, ready to resurface in both old and new manifestations. A 'radical' solution that truly gets to the root of the matter is essential.

As a result of our covenant unity in Adam, all men and women enter the world guilty and corrupt, covenant breakers liable to the holy and just wrath of God. The human condition may be described as one of 'original sin'. In the Westminster Standards this term is used to cover both guilt and corruption, as for example in *Larger Catechism* question 25 and *Shorter Catechism* question 18.

Some Reformed theologians adopt this terminology whilst others refer it only to our inherent corruption. It does mean that in reading these writers care is needed so that we understand precisely what they are saying, but the terminology is less important than the description of the human plight in terms of guilt and pollution/corruption.

It is clear from Scripture that all men and women are born as guilty sinners. David's statement in Psalm 51:5 does not describe a history unique to him: it applies to every individual. 'Behold I was brought forth in iniquity, and in sin did my mother conceive me'. The sin is David's, not that of his mother. Thus the root of sin is present at conception, the first moment of human existence. This is confirmed in the New Testament by Paul's description of pre-conversion humanity in Ephesians 2:1, 3, 'you were dead in the trespasses and sins in which you once walked…and were by nature children of wrath, like the rest of mankind'.

The biblical description of fallen human nature shows that not only is there 'original guilt' inherited from Adam, there is also a comprehensive 'original pollution'. Human beings have lost the original righteousness possessed by Adam and Eve in Eden and in its place is a positive evil which inclines each human being inevitably towards sin. Thus the *Shorter Catechism* refers to 'the want of original righteousness and the corruption of his whole nature' (Q. 18). Both elements must be taken into account: sin is not just an absence of holiness, it includes a positive bias towards evil.

The full seriousness of sin needs to be recognised. Sin is not just a 'disease' of the soul, a spiritual sickness requiring spiritual medicine. When considered in all its aspects, sin is seen to be a spiritual deadness, pervading the whole person. Theologically this may be described as 'total depravity'. The meaning of this term is not that man is in every respect as evil as he could be—that would be 'absolute depravity'—but rather that in no respect is man as good as he should be. In every aspect of his being—his thoughts, his words and his actions—man is ruled by sin and so everything he does is tainted. Even efforts to please God, when done in one's own strength, are sinful and so, as Isaiah says 'all our righteous deeds are like a polluted garment' (Isa. 64:6). 'Total' refers to the extent, not the degree, of depravity. God graciously restrains the full expression of man's sin in this present life.

Attempts to satisfy God's requirements and so 'save ourselves' are also sins that require repentance and forgiveness. They are tokens of our sinful pride and (supposed) self-sufficiency.

One corollary of total depravity is 'total inability'. This is a way of saying that sinners are completely unable to do anything that meets with the approval of God, they cannot change their basic preference for sin and self, and they are unable to come to God in their own strength. Jeremiah states the problem by means of a rhetorical question: 'Can the Ethiopian change his skin or the leopard his spots? Then also you can do good who are accustomed to do evil' (Jer. 13:23). Christ Himself spells out the sinner's inability in John 3:5, 'unless one is born of water and the Spirit, he cannot enter the kingdom of God' and in John 8:34, 'everyone who commits sin is a slave to sin'. Paul states the same truth in Romans 8:7-8: 'the mind that is set on the flesh is hostile to God, for it does not submit to God's law; indeed it cannot. Those who are in the flesh cannot please God'. Our fallenness also expresses itself in an unwillingness to obey God. We are unable and unwilling.

That is not to deny that sinners can do good in some senses. In relation to others, such as their families, they can do many good things that are praiseworthy. They can be good citizens (sometimes called 'civil righteousness'), and sometimes they may put Christians to shame by their honesty and compassion. At one level these actions can be approved of, and people would be worse sinners if they failed to do them. There is, however, a fatal flaw in everything that the sinner does: in his fallen condition, nothing he does is done out of love for God or for the glory of God. There is no God-ward reference in any of a sinner's actions and so ultimately before God they are all stained by sin.

Why are some non-Christians more honest and compassionate than some Christians?

Does anything of the image of God remain in fallen man? Some Reformed theologians speak of the image being entirely destroyed, but often they are referring to the image in a restricted sense of moral uprightness. The image of God in the sense described in chapter 1—

capacity for relationship to God and to other human beings—remains to some extent, albeit severely damaged and greatly defaced. James, for example, refers to 'people who are made in the likeness of God' (James 3:9), and there is no suggestion in the context that only regenerate people are in view. Man is still made for relationships, especially with God, but the necessary capacities have been warped. Only by God's grace can the necessary repairs be effected and a living covenant relationship with God be established. The damage inflicted by sin is severe. As Calvin vividly puts it, the image is 'so vitiated and almost blotted out that nothing remains after the ruin except what is confused, mutilated and disease ridden'.[13]

Fallen man's plight is horrendous. He is a free agent in that he can act in accordance with his nature, and so he is morally responsible for his actions. He is not compelled to sin against his will. His fallen nature, however, inevitably expresses itself in specific sins. He stands under the wrath and curse of a holy God as a rebel and covenant breaker.

Only God's grace can save him.

3

UNITED TO CHRIST

Having listened to the 'bad news' regarding human sin
and liability to punishment, we may now give attention
to the 'good news' of God's gracious action to deliver a
vast multitude of sinners from His righteous wrath and
the deserved punishment of their sins. That deliverance
is 'of his mere love and mercy' (*Larger Catechism* Q30): it
is never something that sinners can earn.

To consider the salvation of sinners is to tackle a vast
subject to which theologians have devoted many weighty
tomes. All of the rich, redemptive work of Christ is here,
together with its application to men and women. In the
space available in a 'pocket guide' we must necessarily be
very selective. In this chapter we will think of salvation

in terms of 'covenant', a theme which runs all the way through the Bible and which has already appeared in the Garden of Eden. Thinking about salvation in a covenant way will open up for us the glorious subject of union with Christ.

THE GOD OF COVENANT

The salvation of sinners has its origin before the coming of Christ into the world, indeed even before the creation of the world. As Ephesians 1:4 tells us, the Father 'chose us in [Christ] before the foundation of the world'. In God's eternal plan of salvation we really do see 'amazing grace'.

Many Reformed theologians (although not all) have argued that salvation is rooted in a covenant established within the Trinity. We must of course beware of forcing an idea into the Bible which is not really there, and we have to proceed with great care and reverence. Nevertheless, it does appear that behind man's experience of salvation lies a covenantal arrangement made within the Trinity before time began. God is infinite and outside time, but if this is how He has revealed His plan, then it is the best way for our minds to grasp it. This is usually referred to as the Covenant of Redemption.

It is evident in the Gospel record that Jesus had a deep awareness of fulfilling a mission with which He had been charged: 'I have come down from heaven, not to do my own will but the will of him who sent me' (John 6:38). This involved not losing any of 'all that he has given me' (v. 39) and it is evident that He had been sent to provide salvation for a people given to Him (see also John 17:2,6,9,24). This ties in with the election of Ephesians 1:4.

Notice too the covenant language in a verse like Psalm 89:3, 'I have made a covenant with my chosen one; I have sworn to David my servant'. Whilst the immediate context is God's covenant with David in 2 Samuel 7:12-14, the quotation of the passage in Hebrews 1:5 shows that the ultimate reference is to the Lord Jesus Christ. The same is true of Isaiah 42:6, 'I have given you as a covenant for the people, a light for the nations', the language used by Simeon in Luke 2:32 with reference to the infant Jesus. We have previously noted the language of covenantal representation used of Adam and of Christ in Romans 5:12-19 and 1 Corinthians 15:22. As Adam was the head of the human race by the Covenant of Works, so Christ was constituted the head of His elect people by the Covenant of Redemption.

Michael Horton succinctly summarises the Covenant of Redemption in this way: 'the Father elects a people in the Son as their Mediator to be brought to saving faith by the Spirit'.[14]

This covenant made before time began unfolds in history in what is usually termed the Covenant of Grace. At the heart of this covenant which God graciously and sovereignly establishes with sinners is the promise found, for example, in Leviticus 26:12, 'I will walk among you and will be your God, and you shall be my people'. The covenant thread can be traced all the way through the

Bible, holding Genesis 17:7 (Abraham) together with Revelation 21:3 (New Creation). God's saving plan is revealed in covenant terms.

The central promise of the Covenant of Grace is of a new relationship with God as a result of the redeeming work of Christ. He is the Mediator of the covenant who deals with sin and provides every blessing God's people will receive. This is the fruit of eternal love to the totally undeserving and so is truly a Covenant of Grace. In covenantal union with Christ His people receive all the blessings He has secured, including justification, adoption and sanctification, leading to resurrection and glorification. As the expression of God's infinite love, the Covenant of Grace cannot fail to reach its ordained goal: nothing can separate believers from God's love in Christ (Rom. 8:38-39).

 What are some of the blessings of understanding that our salvation has its origins in God's plan before the world was even created?

CHRIST OUR REPRESENTATIVE

God's covenant is a 'bond of love' involving love and law, as we saw in chapter 1. It involves much more than legal considerations, but it does include a vital legal dimension. God cannot be in loving fellowship with those who are under the curse of the broken law 'in Adam'. Hence the need for the redemptive work of Christ who is, in Sinclair Ferguson's striking phrase, 'Adam in reverse'.[15]

As Romans 3:26 states, God's provision in Christ 'was to show his righteousness at the present time, so that he might be just and the justifier of the one who has faith in Jesus'. God would deny Himself if He admitted covenant-breakers into fellowship with Himself without addressing their sin in perfect justice.

Mention of justification takes us into the realm of law courts and legal proceedings, and so justification is described as 'forensic'. In both Old and New Testaments it is clear that 'justification' is declarative—a statement about a person's standing before the law. That is evident in Deuteronomy 25:1 and in Matthew 12:37 Jesus contrasts justification and condemnation. Justification of sinners states that in the court of heaven they are righteous in relation to God's law. Their status is 'righteous'. They are declared righteous, not made personally righteous. The latter condition is dealt with in regeneration, which makes them spiritually alive, and sanctification, which makes them holy.

It is a common objection that justification is a 'legal fiction', meaning that God pretends that people who are in fact unrighteous are righteous, a kind of 'let's pretend', unworthy of a holy God. In response two things can be said.

One is that when God justifies sinners there is a righteousness which He takes into account in making His declaration. It is not the righteousness of sinners—who have none—but the righteousness of Christ, which we will consider in a moment.

The second thing to be said is that when God declares a sinner righteous, He thereby constitutes him righteous as far as his legal standing is concerned. The declaration is not a fiction. God's act of justification is constitutive as well as declarative. He does not say that those who are justified are something that they are not. They are constituted righteous as far as their standing in relation to God's law is concerned. Thus Paul in Romans 5:19 says 'by the one man's obedience the many will be made righteous' and this must be linked with his reference to 'the free gift of righteousness' in verse 17. God constitutes His people righteous and then passes the appropriate verdict on them—not merely 'not guilty' but positively 'righteous'. They will subsequently be made righteous in heart and life by the Holy Spirit's work of sanctification.

If we are to understand the role played in salvation by the righteousness of Christ, we need to think of His role as our representative in covenant terms.

Justification changes a sinner's standing in relation to God's law, not his personal condition of sinfulness: the latter is changed by sanctification.

The parallels and contrasts between Adam and Christ set out in Romans 5 take us to the heart of the matter. Both act as our representative in a covenantal capacity. Union with Adam brings death and separation from God. If men and women are to be restored to covenant fellowship with God, their sinful covenant-breaking must be addressed. The covenant-breaking of the first man (and of all mankind) is covered by the covenant-keeping of 'the last Adam' (1 Cor. 15:45). In undertaking in the Covenant of Redemption to save those whom the Father gave Him, the Son committed Himself to the path of obedience, keeping perfectly the law of God, specifically the requirements of the Covenant of Works, as well as the bearing of the sins of His people who have broken the covenant. The righteousness that is necessary for justification is provided by Christ for all those who are 'in him', united to Him by covenant.

REDEMPTION ACCOMPLISHED

The most basic way of understanding the work of Christ by which sinners are saved is in terms of 'obedience'. Theologians usually speak of two aspects to Christ's obedience—'passive' and 'active'. Now we have to bear in mind that Christ was never truly 'passive', the helpless victim of external forces. Even on the cross He was sovereign: 'No one takes [my life] from me, but I lay it down of my own accord' (John 10:18). Nevertheless, the terms do point to the two crucial elements of Christ's obedience.

Christ's Passive Obedience

Christ bore the full penal consequences of the sins of all those chosen in Him in eternity. Thus He can say that as Son of Man He came 'to give his life as a ransom for many' (Mark 10:45). This perspective informs Old Testament passages such as the portrayal of the Suffering

Servant who was 'wounded for our transgressions …
crushed for our iniquities' (Isa. 53:5) and New Testament
passages such as 1 Peter 1:18-19 'you were ransomed
… with the precious blood of Christ, like that of a
lamb without blemish or spot'. The representative,
substitutionary nature of His suffering is clear in a text
such as Galatians 3:13, 'Christ redeemed us from the
curse of the law by becoming a curse for us'.

Christ's Active Obedience

Christ rendered full and perfect obedience to every
requirement of God's law. In Eden Adam as the head
of the human race in the Covenant of Works was under
obligation to render such obedience to the law. The Fall
has not abolished that requirement for all who are 'in
Adam'. The 'lawlessness' that defines sin in 1 John 3:4
includes not only the breaking of particular commands
but also the failure to meet the law's requirements. If
sinners are to be restored to fellowship with God, perfect
obedience is required yet they are unable to supply it.

This underlines the crucial importance of the active
(or 'preceptive') obedience of Christ. At His baptism,
in response to John's reluctance, He stated the necessity
for this action: 'Let it be so now, for thus it is fitting
to fulfil all righteousness' (Matt. 3:15). Throughout His
public ministry He testified to His delight in obeying
His Father's commands as He fulfilled 'all righteousness'.

As the covenant head of His people Christ rendered
full and willing obedience to God's law throughout His

life. He was 'born under the law. To redeem those who were under the law' (Gal. 4:4). Nothing less than perfect obedience was required. Thus he could testify, 'For I have come down from heaven, not to do my own will but the will of him who sent me' (John 6:38)

It is in this context that Romans 5:12-21 is to be understood. One covenant head, Adam, was disobedient and brought death for all who are 'in him'. The other covenant head, Christ, was obedient and brought life for all who are 'in him'. Sinners will in Christ be declared righteous because Christ's obedience satisfies divine justice and provides the righteousness which the 'works of the law' (Rom. 3:20) never could. In Christ there is 'the grace of God and the free gift by the grace of that one man Jesus Christ' (Rom. 5:15). Christ by His full obedience has dealt with the penalty of the broken law and also with the need for perfect law-keeping.

CHRIST THE JUSTIFIED ONE

Every spiritual blessing that believers receive is 'in Christ' (Eph. 1:3). Believers are united in covenant with Christ crucified and risen. We can describe the outworking for believers of that union in this way: union with Christ entails a saving replication in the life-experience of the believer of what has already taken place in the life experience of Christ, the One to whom he is united, namely death and resurrection. The believer dies and rises with Christ, the foundation for every aspect of salvation.[16]

Christ's bodily resurrection includes within it His own justification (1 Tim. 3:16), adoption (Rom. 1:4) and sanctification (Rom. 6:9-11). Justification concerns us here; we will consider adoption and sanctification in due course. The pattern is humiliation followed by exaltation. To speak of Christ 'justified in/by the Spirit' (Rom. 1:4) points to His relationship to the Spirit-wrought act of re-creation that is His resurrection. He is the first participant in the new order of glory and imperishability that Paul describes in 1 Corinthians 15:42-49. Christ's resurrection, understood as His justification, places Him, as the last Adam, in full possession of eschatological righteousness: the Father declared His Son righteous.

When Christ died as a substitutionary sacrifice for His people, He bore the just wrath and curse of God upon the sins of His people. This is clear in texts such as Romans 3:24-25, 2 Corinthians 5:21 and Hebrews 9:26-28. When He was 'made sin' the judicial verdict of guilt was pronounced upon Him, a verdict reversed at the resurrection by the Father's judicial verdict of justification. By His obedience, active and passive, He had satisfied the demands of the broken Covenant of Works. All the demands of divine justice arising from man's covenant-breaking have been met by Christ, both in regard to the positive precept of the law and also to the penal sanction. The risen Christ is declared 'righteous' in God's sight.

Christ crucified and risen contains in Himself every blessing of salvation (see e.g. 1 Cor. 1:30). In Christ is to be found the full, rich, multi-faceted reality of salvation. In Him there is righteousness, sanctification and redemption.

Christ's obedience unto death and consequent resurrection have absolutely decisive significance for believers. He was 'delivered up for our trespasses and raised for our justification' (Rom. 4:25). The resurrection is the divine declaration. By virtue of covenant union with Him, Christ's people are comprehended in that event. As sharers in the Covenant of Grace through faith in Christ they may now 'walk in newness of life' (Rom. 6:4), restored to the place of fellowship with God that was lost in Adam. Everything that the obedience of Christ has secured is counted as belonging to those who are in Him. Once again covenant fellowship with God is a reality. Justification is foundational to that relationship.

We must not lose sight of our union by faith with Christ our covenant head and representative, otherwise we will lose sight of the heart of the gospel.

JUSTIFIED IN CHRIST

Justification was one of the key issues at stake in the Reformers' debate with Rome. For Rome, justification is something God does in us and infused righteousness is crucial. For the Reformers justification is something God does for us, a constitutive declaration on the basis of righteousness external to us.

Drawing on what we have learned of Christ our Representative in the Covenant of Grace, we can say that the basis on which a sinner is justified before God is not anything in himself but solely the righteousness of Christ which is counted by God as belonging to those who are 'in Christ'. They receive the gift of what has been termed an 'alien righteousness'.

Here we are using the language of 'imputation', drawing for example on Romans 4:6, 'David also speaks of the blessing of the one to whom God counts righteousness apart from works'. The verb Paul uses (*logidzesthai*) has the sense of 'count, reckon, impute' and the idea is of something external being credited to the sinner's account. This is the third strand of imputation in the New Testament: the sin of Adam is imputed to those 'in him', the sin of the elect is imputed to Christ and finally the righteousness of Christ is imputed to those 'in him'. Justification involves 'the righteousness of God through faith in Jesus Christ for all who believe' (Rom. 3:22). The result of Christ's being made sin for us is 'that in him we might become the righteousness of God' (2 Cor. 5:21).

Those who reject the first strand of imputation, perhaps because of its supposed 'unfairness', should, to be consistent, reject the second and third strands.

It is the righteousness of Christ in its fullest sense—active and passive—that is counted as belonging to His people. Justification entails the forgiveness of sin on the basis of Christ's redemptive suffering (His 'passive' obedience) and also positive righteousness on the basis of His life of perfect holiness (His 'active' righteousness).

Every aspect of the plight of covenant breakers is completely addressed.

As the Reformers saw clearly, sinners are justified by grace through faith:

1. By grace: as Paul states in Romans 3:24 we are 'justified by his grace as a gift through the redemption that is in Christ Jesus'. The New Testament depicts a clear antithesis between the principle of grace and the principle of works. The two cannot coexist: 'if it is by grace, it is no longer on the basis of works; otherwise grace would no longer be grace' (Rom. 11:6).

2. Through faith: union with Christ is a faith-union and justification is through faith alone. Luther was theologically correct in translating Romans 3:28 as 'by faith alone', adding a word absent from the Greek. In the previous verses Paul indicates that Christ and His propitiation are 'to be received by faith' (v. 25) and that God is 'the justifier of the one who has faith in Jesus' (v. 26). As Ephesians 2:8-9 indicates, even faith is God's gracious gift.

THE IMPORTANCE OF ADOPTION

In the view of John Murray, 'it is adoption into the family of God as sons and daughters of the Lord God Almighty that accords to the people of God the apex of blessing and privilege'.[17] That is fully consistent with Paul's statement of the goal of redemption in Galatians 4:4-5: 'But when the fullness of time had come, God sent forth his Son, born of woman, born under the law, to redeem those who were under the law, so that we might receive adoption as sons'. The highest goal of predestination, according to Ephesians 1:4-5, is adoption: 'In love he predestined us for adoption through Jesus Christ according to the purpose of his will'.

It is significant that in Luke 3:38 Adam is described as 'the son of God'. That status has been lost in the Fall, but membership of the family of God is restored for those who are in union with Christ. Frequently in the Old Testament Israel is described as God's son—Moses was told to say to Pharaoh, 'Israel is my firstborn Son, and I say to you, "Let my son go that he may serve me"' (Exod. 4:22-23). Sonship in the Old Testament is fundamentally redemptive. Thus in Hosea 11:1 God says, 'When Israel was a child, I loved him, and out of Egypt I called my son'. To describe the result of His redeeming work God uses the language of a father carrying his son (Deut. 1:31). That father-son relationship expressed covenant love, as Deuteronomy 7:8 indicates. The Exodus was rooted in God's covenant-keeping. The stage is set for the son.

JESUS THE SON

The Old Testament makes clear that sonship/adoption and covenant are closely interwoven. At Jesus' baptism at the Jordan He hears the Father's voice: 'this is my beloved Son, with whom I am well pleased' (Matt. 3:17).

As He enters upon His redemptive mission culminating at the cross, Jesus is encouraged by His Father in words full of Old Testament significance. They draw on Psalm 2:7, addressed to the messianic King, and on Isaiah 42:1, the opening of one of the songs of the Suffering Servant, and perhaps also on Genesis 22, when Abraham's son Isaac is spared.

Jesus stands at the Jordan as the God-man, perfect in deity and humanity, the representative of His people in the Covenant of Grace, and it is as Son that He acts. Note Jesus' response when John hesitates to baptise Him: 'thus it is fitting for us to fulfil all righteousness' (Matt. 3:15). Jesus as representative of His people will fulfil all the requirements of God's covenant, in particular the Covenant of Works we have broken. He provides the obedience Adam failed to supply. It is as Son He fulfils His mission with the goal 'that we might receive adoption as sons' (Gal. 4:5). Covenant, union and adoption come together.

As we noted previously in quoting Lane Tipton, union with Christ reproduces in God's people the saving significance of His death and resurrection, in particular justification, adoption and sanctification. Jesus is of course not adopted—He is Son eternally by nature. Nevertheless we do see in Romans 1:4 that the resurrection was of great significance for His sonship. As commentators like John Murray and Thomas Schreiner[18] have argued, the best translation is not 'declared' but rather 'appointed'. Here is His appointment, in consequence of His redemptive work, as messianic King, and it is as 'Son of God with power' (these words should be taken together) that He is appointed. The exalted Son reigns as Lord and Christ, and by virtue of their union with Him, God's people share in His sonship by adoption. Having made 'the founder of their salvation perfect through suffering', God works out His purpose of 'bringing many sons to glory' (Heb. 2:10). It is amazing to hear that Christ 'is not ashamed to call them brothers' (v. 11).

ADMISSION TO THE FAMILY

Adoption transfers sinners from a rebellious family into the family of God. It is fundamentally a change of status, and so, like justification, it is a forensic, declarative act, addressing our alienation from God. We have the status of adopted sons. It cannot be separated from justification: indeed it presupposes justification.

As with justification, so with adoption, we must emphasise that this is not a legal fiction, God pretending that something is the case when in fact it is not so. The apostle John marvels at God's bestowal of love such that 'we should be called children of God; and so we are' (1 John 3:1), and he reiterates the point—'Beloved, we are God's children now' (v. 2). As a covenantal act adoption is both legal and relational: God's declaration brings into being the state of affairs He decrees. We are not simply declared to be children of God: that warm, loving family relationship is actually conferred upon us. The forensic is effective. We leave court (justification) to move into the family (adoption).

How is sonship by adoption related to the 'new birth'? Some have regarded these as entirely separate concepts (though compatible) whilst others have in a confusing way drawn indiscriminately on texts relating to both. It is best to regard the two as interrelated inseparably. Not only does God confer on justified sinners the rights and privileges of sons and daughters (adoption), He also ensures that they have the nature matching their status (regeneration, new birth). Those brought into the family are graciously given the new nature appropriate to God's children.

OUR FATHER IN HEAVEN

The Covenant of Grace reveals the love of the Triune God: the love of the Father, the love of the Son and the love of the Holy Spirit for undeserving sinners. With respect to adoption, it is particularly the love of the Father that it emphasised in Scripture.

Adoption is a wonderful demonstration of the Father's love for sinners. Even in translation we can hear the amazement of John when he writes, 'See what kind of love the Father has given to us, that we should be called children of God; and so we are' (1 John 3:1). He adopts us as children in union with Christ. Through the obedience of Christ, active and passive, all the legal obstacles have been removed and the elect may now receive the status of adopted children. The status of Christ, as the eternal Son, is of course unique and the relationship He enjoys with the Father cannot be shared with anyone else. Nevertheless, because we are 'in Christ', the Father views and treats us as beloved children, seeing us as we are in union with the Son. It is a privilege to be treasured and never underestimated. It is also a powerful stimulus to holy living: 'if you call on him as Father who judges impartially according to each one's deeds, conduct yourselves with fear throughout the time of your exile' (1 Pet. 1:17). We are to be holy as He is holy (v. 16).

Sonship is not a status conferred on those who successfully imitate their Father nor is obedience a condition of retaining our Father's love. We obey and pursue holiness as a loving covenant response to His love (1 John 4:19). Adoption liberates us from the 'performance treadmill' of working to remain beloved children.

THE SPIRIT OF ADOPTION

The role of the Holy Spirit in adoption must not be overlooked. Not only is it the Spirit who, by His regenerating work, brings the elect into saving, covenantal union with Christ, He is the one who indwells the adopted children of God; 'he dwells with you and will be in you' (John 14:17). According to Ephesians 1:14, He is 'the guarantee of our inheritance', an important use of legal, sonship language, whilst in the previous verse we are said to be 'sealed with the promised Holy Spirit' (v. 13). He confirms our status as children of God.

This is expressed most powerfully in terms of the experience described in Romans 8. We read in verse 15: 'you have received the Spirit of adoption as sons, by whom we cry Abba, Father'. The Spirit enables us to enjoy the warmth and intimacy of covenant fellowship with God as adopted children. The Spirit also 'bears witness with our spirit that we are children of God' (v. 16). It seems best to understand this expression as a reference to direct testimony 'with our spirit', enabling believers to recognise their Father in many ways—reading His Word, praying, seeing the fruit of His grace in their lives. Thus they cry, 'Abba'.

ALREADY AND NOT YET

The preaching of Jesus recorded in the Gospels centres on the Kingdom of God, declaring that already the Kingdom has come in His person and work, but not yet in the final glory ushered in at His return. This same dynamic applies to our adoption. Already we are adopted as children, in union with Christ (1 John 3:1) but we do not yet experience the full glory God has in store for us. In Romans 8 Paul describes how 'the creation waits with eager longing for the revealing of the sons of God' (v. 19) and connects the creation's groaning for liberation 'from its bondage to decay' with it's sharing in 'the freedom of the glory of the children of God' (v. 21). Paul goes on to say, 'we ourselves, who have the firstfruits of the Spirit, wait eagerly for adoption as sons, the redemption of our bodies' (v. 23). We are united to Christ as persons with bodies, we are adopted as complete people and we will be glorified as complete people. When Christ returns, covenant fellowship with God will be consummated and His children will share in resurrection glory. Being fully like their elder brother (1 John 3:2), their adoption will be complete. The 'not yet' will surely come.

CHRIST OUR SANCTIFICATION

Saved sinners are not only given a righteous standing before God (in justification), they are also made actually holy in the gradual process of sanctification. The two are inseparable. To be justified without subsequent sanctification is an impossibility.

Union with Christ is again crucial. Earlier, drawing on Lane Tipton,[19] we argued that union with Christ entails a saving replication in the life-experience of the believer of what has already taken place in the life experience of Christ, the One to whom he is united, namely death and resurrection. Thus Christ's resurrection includes within it His justification, adoption and sanctification, as well as that of all those united to Him.

How resurrection could be the 'sanctification' of one who was 'a lamb without blemish or spot' (1 Pet. 1:19) is explained in Romans 6:1ff. Believers have died and been raised with Christ and, as a result, 'you must consider yourselves dead to sin and alive to God in Christ Jesus' (v. 11). As the covenant surety of His people Christ has paid the price of redemption, bearing their sin and guilt, and so 'death no longer has dominion over him' (v. 9).

The significance of this for His people is made clear in verse 11. Christ's having died to sin and living to God provides the pattern for believers in their having died to sin and living to God. As the Puritan Walter Marshall puts it, 'His resurrection was our resurrection to the life of holiness…by union with Christ, we partake of that spiritual life that he took possession of for us at his resurrection, and thereby we are enabled to bring forth the fruits of it.'[20]

We are now moving from 'Christ for me' to 'Christ in me'. As Paul puts it in Galatians 2:20, 'I have been crucified with Christ. It is no longer I who live, but Christ who lives in me'. He takes our sinful identity and in its place gives us His holy identity. The Covenant of Grace embraces not only the legal/forensic but also the experiential. Those made alive with Christ will necessarily seek holiness. Union with Christ is not merely the starting point for holiness: it is the source of power for an ongoing life of holiness. Our holiness flows from Him as our new identity in Christ comes to expression in our daily living.

DEFINITIVE SANCTIFICATION

In 1 Corinthians 6:11, Paul says of believers, 'you were washed, you were sanctified'. How are we to reconcile such a statement with our ongoing struggles with temptation and sin? Without denying the necessity for lifelong transformation, we must also grasp the Bible's assertion that the covenant people of God, united to

Christ are already sanctified. This is the precious truth of 'definitive sanctification'.

Passages such as Romans 6:1ff indicate that those united to Christ in His death and resurrection have been delivered from the enslaving power of sin. Paul says they are those 'who died to sin' (v. 2) and they 'have died with Christ' (v. 3). The result is that 'you must also consider yourselves dead to sin and alive to God in Christ Jesus' (v. 11). Union with Christ destroys union with sin. Christ has broken the power of Satan over the elect and the dominating power of sin is consequently broken in all who are in Christ. The decisive blow was struck at Calvary, although the elect do not receive the benefits until conversion. Until then they remain 'children of wrath' (Eph. 2:3).

Paul uses the language of crucifixion in Galatians 2:20 ('I have been crucified with Christ') and Romans 6:6 ('our old self was crucified with him'). What has been crucified is dead. It is unhelpful, therefore, to speak of Christians as having two natures, an old and a new. This obscures the decisive nature of what has taken place because of union with Christ. Much sin certainly remains in believers—old ways, old habits, old weaknesses—but they are 'new' men, not perfect, but those in whom the

In Romans 6:14 Paul says that 'sin shall have no dominion over you'. That is a statement and a promise. We will not return to prison. How do those words help us in the battle with temptation and sin?

dominion of sin has been broken. A new act of creation has taken place (2 Cor. 5:17).

PROGRESSIVE SANCTIFICATION

1 John 1:8 reminds God's covenant people that, 'If we say we have no sin, we deceive ourselves, and the truth is not in us'. Deliverance from the dominion of sin (definitive sanctification) does not end the practice of sin in heart and life, and so progressive sanctification is essential.

To commit sin is to break our covenant obligation to be the Lord's holy people. Such sin is still sin in a Christian, deserving God's holy wrath, and it can be dealt with in only one way. The atoning blood of the Saviour is required, the blood of the Mediator to whom we are united. The good news is that 'the blood of Jesus his son cleanses us from all sin' (1 John 1:7): a repeated and continuous cleansing. God 'is faithful and just to forgive our sins and to cleanse us from all unrighteousness' (v. 9). He is 'faithful' to His covenant promises of forgiveness to the repentant and 'just' in forgiving on the basis of Christ's redeeming work.

Progressive sanctification in union with Christ entails a reproduction in us of the holiness of our covenant Head. Paul's pastoral concern for the Galatians was that 'Christ is formed in you' (Gal. 4:19) and our transformation is 'into the same image, from one degree of glory to another' (2 Cor. 3:18). This is evident from the description of 'the fruit of the Spirit' in Galatians 5:22-23, where each element is exemplified in the Saviour. As He emphasises in the language of the vine and the branches in John 15, only in living union with Him is fruit produced.

This transformation of God's people is bound up with the ministry of the Holy Spirit; the Covenant of Grace is a Trinitarian covenant. The transformation described in 2 Corinthians 3:18 'comes from the Lord who is the Spirit'. It is the Spirit who applies the redeeming work of Christ in sanctification and the resulting Christ-like character is truly 'the fruit of the Spirit' (Gal. 5:22). His role is critical.

COVENANTAL OBEDIENCE

God's people cannot be passive in sanctification. The grace and strength He supplies must be used: 'you also be holy in all your conduct' (1 Pet. 1:15). Thus activity, vigorous Spirit-empowered activity, is necessary for sanctification. Like justification, sanctification is by faith alone: 'the life I now live in the flesh I live by faith in the Son of God who loved me and gave himself for me' (Gal. 2:20). It is a faith expressed in obedient actions.

Sanctification is a comprehensive work, embracing every aspect of life, touching thoughts, emotions and actions. Paul's exhortation is 'let us cleanse ourselves from every defilement of body and spirit, bringing holiness to completion in the fear of God' (2 Cor. 7:1). It is both negative and positive:

1. Mortification: 'if by the Spirit you put to death the deeds of the body, you will live' (Rom. 8:13). The desire to be done with sin is matched by action.

2. Vivification: putting on new spiritual clothing, beginning with desires and inclinations and working into every area of life, the picture used in Colossians 3.

God's promise regarding the New Covenant was, 'I will put my law within them, and I will write it on their hearts' (Jer. 31:33). In union with Christ, keeping God's law is a joyful, loving activity (John 14:15), not a burden (1 John 5:3). The covenant law of God is our guide for a life of obedience.

Justification and definitive sanctification provide the basis for progressive sanctification. We do not ask 'Why bother if we are already sanctified?' As Bryan Chapell says, 'those who are truly in union with Christ increasingly have the desires of the Author of that union, since his heart beats within them'.[21] Ahead is the certainty—'when he appears, we shall be like him' (1 John 3:2).

4

SHARING CHRIST'S GLORY

For the people of God—His covenant community—the best is still to come. Whilst the blessings conferred on believers on account of their covenant union with the Lord Jesus Christ are wonderful, we cannot ignore the statement of Paul in 1 Corinthians 15:19, 'If in Christ we have hope in this life only we are of all people most to be pitied'. To have committed everything to Christ and to have endured the trials of discipleship that come to us in the providence of God, yet to have nothing beyond life in a fallen world where we still wrestle with temptation and sin, would indeed be pitiable. But that is not all we have!

God is the one 'who works all things according to the counsel of his will' (Eph. 1:11). The plans of this sovereign

God cannot fail to be fulfilled. There is nothing outside the comprehensive scope of His sovereignty, even the fall of the sparrows (Matt. 10:29). Thus God's Covenant of Grace cannot fail to reach its ordained goals—ultimately the glory of God—and so, as far as individual believers are concerned, Paul could write, 'I am sure of this, that he who began a good work in you will bring it to completion at the day of Jesus Christ' (Phil. 1:6). We are entering the realm of 'eschatology', the 'last things', which culminate in the new creation where we share Christ's glory.

Why are we to be pitied if we have hope in Christ only in this life?

FACING DEATH

Benjamin Franklin believed that death and taxes are certainties. There may be ways of avoiding taxes, but there is no way finally to avoid death. Modern medicine allied to technology may promise extended life spans, but sooner or later their efforts will be defeated. The process of aging and dying may be slowed, but it cannot be stopped. All must reckon with the inevitability of death.

Despite what some claim, death is not a 'natural' end to life. In chapter 2 we noted how death has come into God's good creation as a result of human sin. As Paul states in Romans 5:12, 'sin came into the world through one man, and death through sin, and so death spread to all men because all sinned'. Death is in fact profoundly unnatural and it is our sinfulness that makes death fearful, that gives death its 'sting' (1 Cor. 15:56). Death may on occasion bring release from suffering, but fundamentally it is the 'last enemy' (1 Cor. 15:26).

We need to understand that death is more than a 'natural consequence' of sin, sinful man dying because he has become mortal. In Hebrews 9:27 we are told that 'it is appointed for man to die once'. Appointed by whom? Clearly by God. Death is His judicial sentence on fallen human beings. The consequences of breaking the Covenant of Works in Eden were spelled out clearly by the Lord: 'of the tree of knowledge of good and evil you shall not eat, for in the day that you eat of it you shall surely die' (Gen. 2:17). The outcome was certain. Death was God's judicial verdict, an intruder into His good creation. Adam and Eve died spiritually as soon as they broke the covenant. Physical death followed later, as they returned to the dust. That is the condition of every sinner and, apart from God's grace, they will experience eventually 'the second death' (Rev. 20:6, 14), eternal separation from God.

The good news of the gospel, however, includes Christ's victory over death in all its aspects. As our Representative in the Covenant of Grace Christ has won the victory over sin and over Satan, and consequently over death. He has taken on Himself the sin that lies at the root of death and so Paul in Romans 5:18 can contrast Christ's achievement with that of Adam and state that 'one act of righteousness leads to justification and life for all men'. With reference to the victory over Satan, one aspect of the work of Christ is 'that through death he might destroy the one who has the power of death, that is, the devil, and deliver all those who through fear of death were subject to lifelong slavery' (Heb. 2:14-15). By virtue of their union with Christ His covenant people share in that comprehensive victory.

Christ was able to say, 'I came that they might have life and have it abundantly' (John 10:10). The 'life' that He gives to those united to Him relates to the whole person, just as 'death' infects the whole person. Body and soul are both liberated from bondage to death: both are included in the Lord's wonderful statement in John 11:25-26, 'I am the resurrection and the life. Whoever believes in me, though he die, yet shall he live, and everyone who lives and believes in me shall never die'. For the Christian death is a defeated enemy: 'in Christ shall all be made alive' (1 Cor. 15:22). Without minimising the reality of death, Paul can speak in defiant terms: 'O death, where is your victory?' and conclude with resounding confidence, 'thanks be to God, who gives us the victory through our Lord Jesus Christ' (1 Cor. 15:55, 57).

If Christ has won the victory over death, why do Christians die? Could they not be translated immediately to heaven at the end of their allotted span, like Enoch (Gen. 5:24)? Why must they endure an experience which may entail catastrophic decline and prolonged suffering? We are assured that such hard and testing experiences cannot separate us 'from the love of God in Christ Jesus our Lord' (Rom. 8:38-39) and our union with Christ is not compromised in any way. The only possible conclusion we can draw is that the believer's passing through death serves God's loving purpose for him in ways that no other experience could. Death is no longer a punishment for sin. Christ has taken the penalty in full. It must therefore serve God's purpose of conforming His people fully to the likeness of His Son. Death, along with our preparations for it, is the final step in our sanctification. Note Paul's aim, expressed in Philippians 3:10, 'that I may know him and the power of his resurrection, and may share his sufferings, becoming like him in his death'. Our death is of course not redemptive, but it is sanctifying, as the attractions of sin are further weakened and in death finally destroyed. Sharing in Christ's sufferings is a neglected aspect of union with Him, but by God's grace death ushers into glory. The *Larger Catechism* explains the death of believers thus: 'it is out of God's love, to free them perfectly from sin and misery, and to make them capable of further communion with Christ in glory, which they then enter upon' (Q85).

The Bible never argues for the survival of the human soul/spirit after death but everywhere assumes it. It shows little interest in an abstract concept of 'immortality'. The Greek words often translated as 'immortality'— *athanasia* ('incapable of death') in 1 Corinthians 15:43, 53 and *aphtharsia* ('incapable of corruption') in 1 Corinthians 15:42, 50, 52-54 in fact describe the state of believers after the resurrection, in their new bodies.

AWAITING THE RESURRECTION

Many people are fascinated by alleged accounts of the experiences of those who claim to have gone beyond death and to have returned. Sometimes these are cases of people who were 'dead' for a time, perhaps in the course of surgery or due to a traumatic incident, and they tell stories of bright lights, gentle beings and beautiful places. None of those who claim such experiences were truly dead, however. Some bodily functions may have stopped, but these individuals have not gone beyond death.

What we genuinely know about the condition of those who have died has been revealed to us by God, who is sovereign over death. The Bible does not describe in detail the condition of the unsaved after death—enough is revealed to show how terrible their experience will be. The Bible's focus is very clearly on the state of believers.

At the end of the wonderful eighth chapter of Romans Paul surveys all the factors that might seem to threaten the believer's future welfare and concludes with ringing assurance, 'I am sure that neither death nor life…nor anything else in all creation, will be able to separate us from the love of God in Christ Jesus our Lord' (Rom. 8:38-39). There can be no doubt that the believer who has died is not separated from the covenant love of the Lord even for a moment. The most important fact about Christians who have passed through death is that they are enfolded in the eternal love of God.

The key expression of the apostle in Romans 8:39 is 'in Christ Jesus'. It is language that is found elsewhere in the New Testament, although it was a favourite of Paul's. In Revelation 14:13 we read, 'Blessed are the dead who die in the Lord from now on' an idea that baffles those without Christian hope. This language expresses the truth that lies at the heart of God's saving sinners, the fundamental way in which to understand salvation, namely union with Christ. United to Christ believers have hope beyond death. All that the believer is and all he looks forward to are rooted in that union. He is united to a Saviour who was crucified and raised for him and so, before, during and after death he is 'in Christ'.

Underlying the language of union with Christ, as considered in detail in the previous chapter, is God's Covenant of Grace: 'I will walk among you and will be your God, and you shall be my people' (Lev. 26:12). In His eternal covenant God gives Himself to His people in Christ and takes them to be His own, also in Christ. Because it depends from the very outset on God's grace, the covenant cannot and will not be broken. That is why the people of God can look to the future with unshakeable confidence, both individually and corporately. Thus the status of believers beyond death is exactly what it was in this life: they are God's covenant people in gracious union with Christ.

So where are those who have died 'in Christ'? We can say with confidence that they are in a place of unbroken covenant fellowship with the Lord. Jesus' promise to the repentant thief was, 'Truly, I say to you, today you will be with me in Paradise' (Luke 23:43), and to the disciples in the Upper Room He indicated that His

Our thinking about the future life of Christians (and of non-Christians) must be shaped and limited by what God has revealed in the Bible. If we wander from it into speculation, we are on dangerous ground.

going and preparing a place for them was so that 'where I am you may be also' (John 14:3). Indeed, as Paul says in Philippians 3:20, 'our citizenship is in heaven'. It is as true beyond this life as it is during this life that nothing 'will be able to separate us from the love of God in Christ Jesus our Lord' (Rom. 8:39). The fellowship of the Covenant of Grace is inviolable.

This perspective is reflected in Paul's dilemma in Philippians 1:21-23. Is death preferable to life for one who is in Christ? He expects that 'now as always Christ will be honoured in my body, whether by life or by death' (v. 20). Then he makes this statement of faith: 'For to me to live is Christ, and to die is gain' (v. 21). It is impossible to believe that Paul would prefer an unconscious existence of unknown duration ('soul sleep') to his present, albeit imperfect, conscious communion with Christ. For it to be 'gain' it must involve conscious communion with the Lord. This is confirmed by his comment, 'My desire is to depart and to be with Christ' (v. 23). In the Greek one definite article governs both 'depart' and 'be', showing that these are two aspects of a single experience. To depart is to be with Christ, immediately and with no intervening period of unconsciousness. For the Christian, 'that is far better' (v. 23).

The same lesson is taught in 2 Corinthians 5:1ff. The opening verses offer some exegetical problems: what does Paul mean when he says 'we have a building from God, a house not made with hands, eternal in the heavens' (v. 1) which he contrasts with 'the tent which is our earthly home'? Does he refer to the resurrection body at the last day or to the glorious state of the dead in Christ at present? Perhaps the best view is that of Calvin: 'I prefer to take it that the blessed state of the soul after death is the beginning of this building, but its completion is the glory of the final resurrection'.[22]

Paul expresses the precious hope of the Lord's people beyond death in verses 6-8. Those united to Christ 'would rather be away from the body and at home with the Lord' (v. 8). Paul uses two verbs in the aorist tense to describe the being away from the body and the being at home: the two are coordinate states, such that being away from the body is to be at home with the Lord. At death the transition to glory 'with the Lord' is immediate and the covenant fellowship is unbroken. All that is good and joyful about 'home' will be fulfilled for believers at death. It is a prospect to stir hope and anticipation.

In heaven believers find rest from struggles, trials, failures and sins: 'Blessed…that they may rest from their labours for their deeds follow them' (Rev. 14:13). They praise the Lord, as the Book of Revelation often tells us (e.g. Rev. 7:9) and there is no sin to spoil their heartfelt praise. The best is still to come, however. They are 'unclothed' (2 Cor. 5:4) without their bodies and so they long for vindication and completion. They cry, 'O sovereign Lord, holy and true, how long before you will judge and avenge our blood…?' (Rev. 6:10).

How should this aspect of Christian hope shape our attitude to life and death? How real is the prospect of 'at home with the Lord' to you?

RAISED IN GLORY

It is surprising how many people think that Christians are interested only in souls, with the body regarded as of little value. This in fact is an attitude characteristic of many strands of Greek philosophy in which the bodily and the material were devalued. The body was regarded as a 'tomb' from which escape was sought. Whilst this outlook has sometimes influenced Christians, the biblical outlook could not be more different.

As Genesis 1-2 shows, God is the Creator of all things, including the material and in particular the human body. Originally, like all created things, it was 'very good' (Gen. 1:31). Sin has affected every aspect of human nature including the body: 'you are dust and to dust you shall return' (Gen. 3:19). God's answer to sin also addresses the whole person, the redeeming work of Christ relates to the entire being of His people. Thus Christ 'will save his people from their sins' (Matt. 1:21), not just their souls. Satan will not enjoy a measure of victory by destroying the bodies of believers. God gives value to the body, Christ saves His people's bodies and so the body is to be treated with great respect.

At the heart of the Christian's resurrection hope is his covenant union with Christ: 'For if we have been united with him in a death like his, we shall certainly be united with him in a resurrection like his' (Rom. 6:5). Because we are united to Him by grace, we die to the old life of sin and rise to a new life of holiness. We begin to experience this spiritually now: '[God] raised us up with him and seated us with him in the heavenly places in Christ Jesus' (Eph. 2:6). It will be consummated in our bodily resurrection at the return of the Saviour. As *Shorter Catechism* Q 37 states of believers, 'their bodies, being still united to Christ, do rest in their graves till the resurrection'. There is no possibility that believers will fail to be raised.

In John 5:29 Jesus refers both to 'the resurrection of life' and to 'the resurrection of judgment'. The unsaved will be raised, but only to face judgment and punishment.

In 1 Corinthians 15:20 the risen Christ is 'the firstfruits of those who have fallen asleep'. As 'firstfruits' He is the first part of the harvest that guarantees the gathering of the whole crop. Thus in verse 23 we read, 'But each in his own order: Christ the firstfruits, then at his coming those who belong to Christ'. Because Christ is risen, never to die again, all those united to Him in the Covenant of Grace will also rise. As He says in John 14:19, 'Because I live, you also will live'. The same idea is expressed by Paul in Colossians 1:18 where Christ is designated 'the firstborn from the dead': not only first in order but also the cause of the resurrection of His people.

The Lord himself sets out the great resurrection hope of His people in John 6:40, 'For this is the will of my Father, that everyone who looks on the Son and believes in him should have eternal life and I will raise him up on the last day'. The 'I' is emphatic, stressing that Christ personally will raise up those for whom He died, a glorious testimony to His love. This does not detract from the Trinitarian nature of our resurrection, as the Father also raises us (John 5:21) and it is through the Holy Spirit's agency (Rom. 8:11). The focus, however, is on Christ 'who will transform our lowly body to be like his glorious body, by the power that enables him to subject all things to himself' (Phil. 3:21).

The resurrection is necessary so that believers as whole persons can share in the victory of Christ. The Bible also shows that the resurrection completes believers' adoption. We are presently adopted children of God, as 1 John 3:2 shows, yet not in the fullest sense. The body must be included. Thus Paul writes in Romans 8:23, 'we ourselves, who have the firstfruits of the Spirit, groan inwardly as we wait eagerly for adoption as sons, the redemption of our bodies'. Already believers enjoy the status and privileges of God's adopted children, but not yet in all the richness that will be experienced at the last day. There will, no doubt, be new dimensions to our relationship as we relate to God and serve Him as beloved children body and soul. How it may change from the present may be beyond our comprehension, but the resurrection will complete adoption.

The resurrection also equips the Lord's people for glory. As 1 Corinthians 15:50 states, 'flesh and blood cannot inherit the kingdom of God, nor does the perishable inherit the imperishable'. The present bodies we inhabit are not suitable for the resurrection life. A new kind of life requires a new kind of body, as it did in the case of the Saviour. Our present bodies bear the scars of sin and are returning to the dust (Gen. 3:19), subject to dissolution under the curse of God. In bodily terms we are not equipped for glory but the resurrection will provide the necessary transformation. Even those living at the return of Christ will require transformation: 'We shall not all sleep, but we shall all be changed' (1 Cor. 15:51).

What will the resurrection body be like? It is a subject about which Christians have often wondered, and sometimes speculated. The Bible offers a limited amount of information, perhaps because more would simple baffle our limited capacities. Paul does speak about the resurrection body in 1 Corinthians 15:35ff. The body will be, he indicates, the same as the present one yet profoundly different. He uses the analogy of the seed which must 'die' if the plant is to grow (v. 36). He goes on, 'what you sow is not the body that is to be, but a bare seed' (v. 37). So it is with the resurrection body: we cannot tell from examination of the present body what the nature of the resurrection body will be. There is both continuity and discontinuity, with the resurrection body having a unique heavenly glory (v. 39-41).

Paul then offers four contrasts between the present and the resurrection bodies. 'What is sown is perishable; what is raised is imperishable' (v. 42): the resurrection body will be free from pain and disease, no longer subject to the curse of the broken covenant in Eden (Gen. 3:19). 'It is sown in dishonour; it is raised in glory' (v. 43): there is no glory in the process of aging, sickening and dying, whereas the resurrection body will share in Christ's glory (Phil. 3:21). As the great theologian Francis Turretin puts it, 'it will be nothing less than the irradiation of God's glory, from which these bodies will be made to shine'.[23] Thirdly, 'It is sown in weakness; it is raised in power' (v. 43): the resurrection body, probably in many ways, will transcend the weaknesses and limitations of the present body. Finally, 'It is sown a natural body; it is raised a spiritual body' (v. 44). The 'natural' is what is associated with our fallen nature. The 'spiritual' is not made of spirit—it is material—but is provided by and indwelt by the Holy Spirit, no doubt to a degree never previously experienced. In every respect we will be ready for our new life.

What we know of the resurrection should stir us to present service: 'be steadfast, immovable, always abounding in the work of the Lord' (1 Cor. 15:58).

THE FINAL JUDGMENT

When Paul writes in 2 Corinthians 5:10 that 'we must all appear before the judgment seat of Christ, so that each may receive what is due for what he has done in the body, whether good or evil', he is stating a truth with which every human being must reckon. Although saved and lost are separated at death (Luke 16:22-24), there will nevertheless be a final judgment to display the sovereignty and glory of God in dispensing justice and exercising grace. The judgment will also reveal the degrees of reward and punishment each one deserves, and the place in which each will spend eternity will be fixed. Judgment is a solemn reality.

A view of Christ which omits His role as Judge is seriously defective. As Paul says in Acts 17:31, '[God] has fixed a day on which he will judge the world in righteousness by a man whom he has appointed'. Each one will be judged on the basis of the light of truth available to him and his response to it, whether creation, conscience or the written revelation of God. As Romans 1:20 indicates, even those who have had God's revelation in creation, without His written Word, will be 'without excuse'. The only hope for sinners is to be found in Christ: 'Whoever believes in the Son has eternal life; whoever does not obey the Son shall not see life, but the wrath of God remains on him' (John 3:36). There are only two possibilities.

Those who stand before Christ in their natural fallen condition, apart from the saving grace of God, the 'goats' on Christ's left hand according to Matthew 25:33, will hear from Him the terrible sentence, 'Depart from me, you cursed, into the eternal fire prepared for the devil and his angels' (v. 41). Similarly His verdict recorded in Matthew 7:23 will be, 'I never knew you; depart from me you workers of lawlessness'. For the Lord to 'know' someone indicates a relationship of gracious covenant love; for Him to say 'I never knew you' indicates the complete absence of such grace and love, the entire lack of the relationship which is the very definition of 'life'. Thus at the last day the sinner's covenant breaking reaps its full reward of 'death', as the fulfilment of the sentence threatened in Eden (Gen. 2:17).

Hell is real. No one spoke more about it than Christ Himself. He refers in Matthew 18 to 'the eternal fire' (v. 8) and 'the hell of fire' (v. 9). To submit to His authority requires us to believe in hell. Confinement in hell will be a just punishment for man's covenant breaking: 'God has set a day when he will judge the world with justice' (Acts 17:31, NIV) and Romans 2:5 refers to 'the day of wrath when God's righteous judgment will be revealed'.

Hell is described in the language of fire and the undying worm (e.g. Mark 9:48). Most likely the language is figurative, but, as A. A. Hoekema says, 'If the figures used…do not mean unending suffering, they mean nothing at all'.[24] We need to be clear that the language of 'perishing' in, for example, John 3:16, refers not to annihilation but to 'lostness', as in the case of the coin and the sheep in Luke 15. The term 'eternal' likewise cannot be emptied of its reference to that which is 'unending'. Indeed, as Christ says in Matthew 25:46, the punishment of the lost and the life of the saved are both 'eternal': characteristic of the age to come and unending. However sincerely some argue for annihilation of the lost or for some form of 'conditional immortality', the Bible clearly depicts an eternal hell.

To the 'sheep' on his right hand, however, Christ will say, 'Come, you who are blessed by my Father, inherit the kingdom prepared for you from the foundation of the world' (Matt. 25:34). Those who are in Christ will enter into the full experience of the salvation purchased for

Hell is a solemn doctrine and should always be preached and spoken about with loving concern that sinners will repent and be saved.

them by their Covenant Head. They do not need to fear appearing before the judgment seat of Christ because the Judge has already been judged in their place, bearing the full burden of their sin and guilt. As Paul states in 2 Corinthians 5:21, 'For our sake [God] made him to be sin who knew no sin, so that in him we might become the righteousness of God'. In the judgment believers' sins will be seen only as forgiven sins and all the praise will be to the God of covenant grace. To know that there is now 'no condemnation for those who are in Christ Jesus' (Rom. 8:1) is wonderfully liberating, lifting any burden of guilt or fear.

In addition to the experience of God's reign of grace— 'the kingdom prepared for you from the foundation of the world' (Matt. 25:34)—unspoiled by any sin, the Lord's people will experience too, life in its fullness. Matthew 25:46 says that 'the righteous' will go away 'into eternal life'. What they have begun to enjoy in this world will be theirs, body and soul, after the final judgment as they delight in the life of the Covenant of Grace in all its richness and are, supremely, 'with the Lord for ever' (1 Thess. 4:17). Although they will say, 'We are unworthy servants; we have only done what was our duty' (Luke 17:10), so great is the Lord's love for them that He will shower gracious, undeserved rewards upon them. If their work stands His test (1 Cor. 3:10-15) they will receive a reward. Matthew 25:14-30 indicates that rewards will be proportionate to the outcome of their efforts and are perhaps best thought of as increased capacities to enjoy God and to serve Him. They will be amazed, having performed their service primarily for the glory of God, rather than for the promised rewards (Matt. 25:34ff.). Rewards are promised for the encouragement of believers, yet they are not at the forefront of their minds as they serve the Lord. At the Last Day they will praise the grace of God that enabled them to serve: 'What do you have that you did not receive?' (1 Cor. 4:7).

THE NEW CREATION

The Lord is not finished with His creation: it will share in the final glory at the return of Christ. In Romans 8:21 Paul refers to our hope 'that the creation itself will be set free from its bondage to decay and obtain the freedom of the glory of the children of God'. It is significant that Paul speaks of this in terms of 'adoption as sons', which he defines as 'the redemption of our bodies' (v. 23). The material creation will share in the glorification of the bodily aspect of believers' existence as body and soul they enjoy the full blessings of being adopted children of God.

In ways beyond our comprehension the Lord will transform the present creation—not annihilate it— to remove all the effects of man's sin and covenant breaking. The damage described in Genesis 3 as a result of God's sentence will be undone on the basis of Christ's redemptive work. 'But according to his [God's] promise we are waiting for new heavens and a new earth in which righteousness dwells' (2 Pet. 3:13). The Lord will provide a suitable home for His saints, redeemed and resurrected. Will they not be in heaven? Indeed they will. Since heaven is where God dwells in grace and glory, the new creation and heaven will become one. In the language of Revelation 21:2, 'I saw the holy city, new Jerusalem, coming down out of heaven from God, prepared as a bride adorned for her husband'. It is no surprise that covenant language is used to describe the scene in Revelation 21:3, 'Behold, the dwelling place of God is with man. He will dwell with them, and they will be his people, and God himself will be with them as their God'. It is covenant life in its fullness.

Much about the new creation lies beyond our understanding, but believers can certainly look forward to eternal embodied life in a world free from sin and full of a beauty that reflects it's Creator. Like Eden, it will surely be full of sound, colour and fragrance, satisfying all our senses. Although it is a 'Sabbath rest' (Heb. 4:9), it will be a rest from labour, trials and suffering, not a rest of inactivity. Like Eden, there will be work to do, all of it fruitful and satisfying. There will always be more to do and more to learn about the Triune God. We might sum up its wonders in 5 words:

1. Righteousness: 'in which righteousness dwells' (2 Pet. 3:13): everything will be in harmony with the righteousness of God, so 'we shall be like him' (1 John 3:2).

2. Fulfilment: free of sin and frustration, believers will be all that God has made them to be, enjoying the perfect home He has provided for them.

3. Fellowship: the centre of the Covenant of Grace is fellowship with God and His people. In the new creation 'they will see his face' (Rev. 22:4) and nothing will detract from that communion. They will dwell in the unity of Psalm 133.

4. Beauty: the language of Revelation 21-22 stresses the beauty of the new creation, a mirror of the Creator's beauty: 'It shone with the glory of God' (Rev. 21:11, NIV).

5. Security: the blessings of the new creation cannot be lost: they have been secured by the blood of Christ. Everywhere Scripture speaks of these glories in the language of certainty. The inheritance is 'imperishable, undefiled and unfading' (1 Pet. 1:4). In a world of insecurity, this is the ultimate security.

 In view of what lies ahead, 'what sort of people ought you to be in lives of holiness and godliness'? (2 Pet. 3:11).

AND FINALLY...

The Bible ends on a note of triumphant joy, which comes as no surprise. The plan of salvation established in the counsels of the sovereign Triune God in eternity will be brought to a glorious conclusion that perfectly fulfils every detail of God's will. At no point does the fulfilment fall short of the plan.

The biblical record has described the work of creation which produced a perfect universe that reveals the glory of its Creator, and at the centre of the creation were placed two human beings made in the image of God and equipped for a covenant relationship of love and service with God. Still within the sovereign will of God, sin entered the creation and wrought horrendous damage as man opted for rebellion against the Creator rather than hearty obedience. The response of the LORD to man's sin was the sending of a Saviour, the eternal Son of God, who would take human nature into union with Himself and in that humanity He would represent those given to Him by divine election. His life of perfect obedience and His atoning death on the cross, followed by His victorious resurrection, provided all that was required for the salvation of a vast multitude of sinners. Brought into a gracious covenant with God, they are gradually remade in the image of Christ, taken to share His glory after death and in resurrected bodies will enjoy the wonders of the new creation at Christ's return. That work of salvation is by God's grace from start to finish. Were they not revealed by God, we would not dare to think such things were possible.

At the heart of this salvation is union with Christ. Made alive by the Holy Spirit, sinners are brought into union with Christ, legally and experientially, in His death and resurrection. They pass from death to life in Him. It is a union that cannot be broken. God's redeemed people are united to their Saviour for ever. Apart from that union there is no possibility of salvation, no hope now or in eternity. In union with Christ there is a rich and full salvation and a hope that will never disappoint, enabling believers to be all that God created them to be.

These are not abstract truths given for impersonal debate in the classroom. They are the great facts of God's dealings with sinners which should impact our lives profoundly.

The terrible consequences of dying outside this union with Christ ought to act as a powerful stimulus to heart-searching: make sure that you are found in Christ by grace through faith. There is no other path to an eternity within the fellowship of the family of God, united to the only Saviour. If you are not united to Christ when you leave this life, you will spend eternity separated from God, experiencing His righteous wrath, without hope of salvation. For you this is a matter of eternal life and eternal death.

Those who are united to Christ in His death and resurrection, who have the prospect of glory ahead of them, should surely be people filled with praise and thanksgiving. We should let an awareness of the abundance of God's grace permeate our lives and rejoice our hearts while we are being conformed to the likeness of the Saviour by the power of the Holy Spirit. Serving this God with all we are and all we have is no burden, but rather a joy and a privilege. We ought to meditate often on these precious truths and seek to feel their power in our lives every day.

FURTHER READING

Thomas Boston, *Human Nature in its Fourfold State*, 1850 edition, (London, 1964).

Bryan Chapell, *Holiness by Grace*, (Wheaton, 2001).

Anthony A. Hoekema, *Created in God's Image*, (Grand Rapids, 1986).

—— *Saved by Grace*, (Grand Rapids, 1989).

Robert Letham, *Union with Christ in Scripture, History and Theology*, (Phillipsburg, 2011).

J. Gresham Machen, *The Christian View of Man*, (London, 1965).

David McKay, *The Bond of Love*, (Fearn, 2001).

K. Scott Oliphant (ed), *Justified in Christ: God's Plan for us in Justification*, (Fearn, 2007).

Robert A. Peterson, *Adopted by God*, (Phillipsburg, 2001).

Richard L. Pratt Jr., *Designed for Dignity*, 2nd edition (Phillipsburg, 2000).

Michael D. Williams, *Far as the Curse is Found*, (Phillipsburg, 2005).

ENDNOTES

1 John Calvin, *Institutes of the Christian Religion*, 1559 edition, translated by Ford Lewis Battles (Philadelphia, 1960), I.iii.1-2.

2 John Calvin, *Commentaries on the First Book of Moses called Genesis*, translated by John King (Grand Rapids, 1948), 1.91.

3 Thomas Watson, *A Body of Divinity*, (Edinburgh, 1965), p. 7.

4 Vaughan Roberts, *Transgender* (Epsom, 2016), p. 30.

5 This is worked out in detail by Wayne Grudem in *Systematic Theology* (Nottingham, 2007), pp. 473-7.

6 This is worked out in detail in David McKay, *The Bond of Love* (Fearn, 2001).

7 Robert Rollock, 'A Treatise of God's Effectual Calling, 1603 edition, translated by H. Holland in *Select Works of Robert Rollock* (Edinburgh, 1849), p. 34.

8 The proposed alternative translations are unsatisfactory. 'Like man/men they have broken the covenant': it is stating the obvious. 'As at Adam they have broken the covenant': no (presumably well-known) covenant breaking at a place called Adam can be suggested.

9 See for example Wayne Grudem, 'Does Kephalē ('Head') Mean 'Source' or 'Authority Over' in Greek Literature? A survey of 2,336 Examples' in *Trinity Journal* 6, n.s. (Spring '85) and 'The Meaning of Kephalē ('Head'): A Response to Recent Studies' in *Trinity*

Journal 11, n.s. (Spring '90) reprinted as Appendix I in *Recovering Biblical Manhood and Womanhood*, eds John Piper and Wayne Grudem (Wheaton, 1991).

10 See Grudem, *Systematic Theology*, pp. 492-3.

11 For fuller consideration of the meaning of Genesis 3:16 see Susan T. Foh, *Women and the Word of God* (Phillipsburg, 1979) chapter III, and Sharon James, *God's Design for Women* (Darlington, 2002), chapter 4. This is the view reflected in the 2016 ESV translation of Genesis 3:16 'Your desire shall be contrary to your husband', but we should note that it is not accepted by all scholars, some of whom do not see a second curse on Eve in the latter part of the verse.

12 John Murray, *The Epistle to the Romans* (Grand Rapids, 1968), p. 204, on Romans 5:19. Murray's comments on the whole passage are most helpful.

13 John Calvin, *Institutes*, I.xv.4.

14 Michael Horton, *God of Promise: Introducing Covenant Theology* (Grand Rapids, 2006), p. 6.

15 Sinclair B. Ferguson, *The Christian Life. A Doctrinal Introduction* (London, 1981), p. 95.

16 This is stated in more technical terms by Lane G. Tipton: 'Union with Christ is a soteric replication in the structure of the believer's life-experience of what happened antecedently in the life experience of Christ, namely death and resurrection'. See Lane G. Tipton, 'Union with Christ and Justification' in *Justified in Christ: God's Plan for Us in Justification*, edited by K. Scott Oliphint (Fearn, 2007), p. 25.

17 John Murray, *Redemption Accomplished and Applied* (Grand Rapids, 1955), p. 170.

18 See the comments on these verses in John Murray, *The Epistle to the Romans*, 1968 edition (Grand Rapids and Cambridge, 1997), and Thomas R Schreiner, *Romans*, Baker Exegetical Commentary on the New Testament (Grand Rapids, 1998).

19 Lane G. Tipton, 'Union with Christ and Justification', p. 25.

20 Walter Marshall, *The Gospel Mystery of Sanctification*, 1692 edition (Grand Rapids, 2015), p. 36.

21   Bryan Chapell, *Holiness by Grace. Delighting in the Joy That is Our Strength* (Wheaton, 2001), p. 50.

22   John Calvin, *The Second Epistle of Paul the Apostle to the Corinthians and the Epistles to Timothy, Titus and Philemon*, translated by T. A. Smail (Edinburgh and London, 1964), p. 67.

23   Francis Turretin, *Institutes of Elenctic Theology*, translated by G M Giger (Phillipsburg, 1992-7), Locus 20, Q9, para 7 (3.619).

24   A. A. Hoekema, *The Bible and the Future* (Exeter, 1979), p. 268.

A Christian's Pocket Guide to Eastern Orthodoxy
Panagiotis Kantartzis

We may associate a number of images with the Eastern
Orthodox church – ornate church buildings, services
with candles and incense, men wearing embellished
robes – but what does the Eastern Orthodox church
actually believe? What are the similarities and differences
between them and western evangelical churches? In
this short book Panagiotis Kantartzis introduces us to
Eastern Orthodoxy and tells us what we need to know.

*... clear, concise and well-researched .... If you want the best
engagement with Orthodoxy from an evangelical perspective,
look no further.*

Michael Horton
J. G. Machen Professor of Systematic Theology
and Apologetics, Westminster Seminary, Escondido,
California

978-1-5271-0641-3

A Christian's Pocket Guide to How We Got the
Bible

Greg Lanier

This short book answers some critical questions about
the Word of God, helping us to understand where
the Scriptures came from and why we can trust them.
Covering the origins and translations of the Old and
New Testaments, this straightforward introduction
answers many questions, and provides suggestions for
further reading if you want to research the topic further.

*Without being overly wordy or technical, this pocket guide
provides clear and accessible explanations for why we can be
confident that our Bibles are the Word of God.*

Nancy Guthrie
Bible teacher and author of *Seeing Jesus in the Old
Testament* series

978-1-5271-0268-2

A Christian's Pocket Guide to How God
Preserved the Bible

Richard Brash

There is sometimes a gap in the teaching we receive
between the inspiration and illumination of Scripture.
The Holy Spirit inspired the writing of the Word of God
in the first place and applies it to our hearts now. How do
we know that the Bible we read today is still the inspired
Word of God? Richard Brash grounds his answers to
these questions in the doctrines of God and His outer
works, especially providence, in this introductory guide
to how God preserved the Bible.

*This is a wonderfully lucid introduction to a much–neglected
doctrine. It will help many to grow in their confidence in the
Bible and in their adoration in the sovereign, speaking God.*
Vaughan Roberts
Rector of St Ebbe's, Oxford and Director of
Proclamation Trust

978-1-5271-0421-1

A Christian's Pocket Guide to Understanding
Suicide and Euthanasia

D. Eryl Davies

In a society that does not like to speak about death,
Eryl Davies brings a contemporary, biblical, pastoral
perspective on one of the most controversial topics of our
times. The desire to control when and how one's life ends
can be a complex and heart–breaking issue, so Davies
encourages Christians to be informed, and to engage
with the debate, bringing God's light to the darkness.

*… will be of great value to those needing immediate guidance
in difficult situations, as well as those who want to start
thinking more deeply about the issues raised by the current
debates on assisted dying, euthanasia and suicide.*

John Alcolado
Executive Dean, Chester Medical School, University of
Chester, UK

978-1-5271-0420-4

A Christian's Pocket Guide to Suffering
Brian H. Cosby

When tragedy strikes-the death of a child, hurricanes, a school shooting-we begin looking for an escape from the pain, a way out, or we clamor for answers from a panel of religious 'experts' to explain the ever-present question, 'Why?' We want answers and we want to believe that our suffering isn't meaningless.

A concisely written, pastorally focused, gospel-infused account of the place of suffering in the Christian life. A perfect guide to aid troubled souls find peace and comfort when the storm breaks.

Derek W. H. Thomas
Senior Minister of Preaching and Teaching,
First Presbyterian Church, Columbia, South Carolina

978-1-7819-1646-9

A Christian Pocket Guide to Mary
Leonardo De Chirico

A Christian's Pocket Guide to Mary offers a biblical account of Mary's character, contrasting this with the Roman Catholic traditions which have developed throughout history, distorting her nature from an obedient servant and worshipper of God to a worshipped saint herself. De Chirico writes with the authority of thorough research as well as personal experience of the traditions surrounding Mary which have become so integral to Roman Catholic worship.

Leonardo De Chirico is one of my most trusted authorities on Roman Catholic doctrine.... In this short book he demonstrates what the Roman Catholic Church teaches about Mary and aptly proves why so much of it is opposed to the plain teaching of the Bible. I heartily commend it to you.

Tim Challies
Blogger at www.challies.com

978-1-5271-0060-2

Christian Focus Publications

Our mission statement —

STAYING FAITHFUL

In dependence upon God we seek to impact the world through literature faithful to His infallible Word, the Bible. Our aim is to ensure that the Lord Jesus Christ is presented as the only hope to obtain forgiveness of sin, live a useful life and look forward to heaven with Him.

Our books are published in four imprints:

CHRISTIAN
FOCUS

Popular works including biographies, commentaries, basic doctrine and Christian living.

CHRISTIAN
HERITAGE

Books representing some of the best material from the rich heritage of the church.

MENTOR

Books written at a level suitable for Bible College and seminary students, pastors, and other serious readers. The imprint includes commentaries, doctrinal studies, examination of current issues and church history.

CF4•K

Children's books for quality Bible teaching and for all age groups: Sunday school curriculum, puzzle and activity books; personal and family devotional titles, biographies and inspirational stories — because you are never too young to know Jesus!

Christian Focus Publications Ltd,
Geanies House, Fearn, Ross-shire,
IV20 1TW, Scotland, United Kingdom.
www.christianfocus.com